THE BOYS I DIDN'T KISS

Also by the author

Maud Gone, a novel
The Last Room in Manhattan, a novel

THE BOYS I DIDN'T KISS AND OTHER ESSAYS

by Kathleen Rockwell Lawrence

British American Publishing

Published by British American Publishing
19B British American Boulevard
Latham, New York 12110

Manufactured in the United States of America

94 93 92 91 90 5 4 3 2 1

Pieces in this collection have appeared in slightly different form in the following publications: American Health Magazine, Glamour Magazine, MS. Magazine, Newsday, New Woman, The New York Times HERS column, 7 Days, Vogue, Parents Magazine, Poets and Writers Magazine, Woman's Day, and Writer's Digest.

"The Nose Job" lyrics by Norman Blagman and Sam Bobrick, Norick Music Inc.

"Dear Ezra, I am Old" By permission of William M. Murphy, Executor of the Estate of Jeanne R. Foster.

Library of Congress Cataloging-in-Publication Data

Lawrence, Kathleen Rockwell.
    The boys I didn't kiss / Kathleen Rockwell Lawrence.
        p.   cm.
    ISBN 0-945167-34-2 : $17.95
    I. Title.
PS3562.A9128B6   1990
814'.54—dc20
                                                                    90-1574
                                                                    CIP

For Paul,
who told me to keep the party going

Contents

THE BOYS
I DIDN'T KISS

The Boys I Didn't Kiss

Twenty-Fifth Reunion Address to the Class of 1963
Wellsville High School
Wellsville, New York
June 18, 1988

I blew the dust of years from my 1963 *Sonnontouan*. Our year-book would be my inspiration for this speech. I tried to remember who I was then, who we were then. I looked at us all, stopped in black-and-white stills of time. Sweet-faced girls in short prim roller sets, teased beneath, smooth on top, wearing our pearls-and-black-drape issue from the photography studio. Clean-cut boys in brush cuts; bad boys with hair swept back in wethead pompadours. To my middle-aged eyes, even the baddest of these boys, the sexiest, the ones who held the most terror for me — I hate to say this — even they look clean-cut and innocent.

Was there some clue to us in our nicknames beneath the pictures? We chose them when we filled in the slot that said "Nickname," so they must define us in some way. What do they mean, nicknames like: Fi-Fi, Kervie, Rotten, Fingers, Worm, Beeps, Casey, The Lover, Haystack, Rabbit, Weevil, and Weasely, Fragile, Nig, Play Boy, Baldie, Pudgie, Rebel, Punkie, Maze, J.B. and B.J., Egghead, Snooks, Gabe, Deac, Nose, Weensie, Kook-a-Leech, Mort, and Taters? What do they mean? I do not know what they mean. Perhaps, though, if you are still using certain of these nicknames...

I looked elsewhere: the activity lists beneath our names, our accomplishments. I wanted to see how we kept busy and prestigious: St. Coun 3; Nat Hon Soc 2; Pep Band 1234; Lat.Cl

3

34; 4-H 234; Orch 2; Fresh Bask B; Base B.; Foot B.; H.R. Off; Movie Op. Cl.; Wrest; FFA; FHA; FTC. Who had the most print? Who had the least? Who didn't give a shit and had none? And what does it mean at this distance? Who gives a shit now?

More enduring listings for us would include: Viet War '64–'75; Assassinations of leaders '63 and '68; Moon '69; Janis Joplin '70; Elvis '77; John Lennon '80; Three Mile Island '79; Chernobyl '86; and such ongoing items as El Salvador, Nicaragua, the Middle East, AIDs. Those who stayed in Wellsville can add to their list the year 1972, and a flood so devastating that the citizens had to wrest a river from its course forever.

Personally our listings might include marriage and divorce, the birth of children, the death of parents, and lately, the deaths of friends, a son or daughter grown and gone.

And so, continuing in my search, I looked at the inscriptions to me that you scribbled across your faces that blistering afternoon at the yearbook party in the Girls Gym, or later on, in Cretekos Sweet Shoppe. "To a real sweet gal," you wrote to me, or "To a really nice girl." "If you go to the lake this summer," Tom Fleming wrote me, "stay out of what everybody else will be into." Tom Fleming knew me well: we'd been classmates together since first grade at Immaculate Conception grammar school. The Sisters of Mercy taught me what to stay out of, and I was a very good student. I was sweet and nice, to my sorrow. I was a good girl of the fifties, and Irish-Catholic besides. I did not make out.

That's what I'll talk about, I thought. The Boys I Didn't Kiss. The world's longest speech. I could tell them how sorry I am, that it wasn't them, it was me. And how sorry I am that I called up Daddy and left Karen Sanford's party when someone brought in two six-packs of Genesee. How sorry that I didn't go out for a soda when Mike Brown invited me. (Instead, I told

him, "I'm not allowed to date.") Mike, forgive me! I really wanted
to! This reunion will be my chance to tell everyone I've changed!
I'm not goody two-shoes any more!

No. A reunion speech cannot be about oneself. It has to be
larger. It has to have a great theme. It can't be about not kissing
boys. Not kissing boys is not a great theme.

So I continued to flip through the *Sonnontouan*, back to front,
looking for a great theme to hang this talk on. At length I arrived at the Wellsville High School crest: two lions sticking
their tongues out at each other standing upon a wavy ribbon
that says, in its wavy way, "High Wellsville School" and above
the lions, over crossed swords, is the motto: "Carpe Diem."

Carpe Diem: Seize the day! Live for the moment! One of the
world's great themes, that tradition of poetry going all the way
back to the orgying Romans, telling us most urgently that life
is short and must be lived. *Now.* If Charlie Fuller had taught
us those poems in senior English instead of *Macbeth*, I might
have had more fun in high school, because mainly what Carpe
Diem means is seize the day about kissing boys.

We hear strains of Carpe Diem in works as disparate as the
Sanskrit's "Look to this Day!"; Janis Joplin's "Get It While You
Can"; and Wordsworth's wonderful "Nothing can bring back
the hour, of splendor in the grass, or glory in the flower."

Nothing will bring them back: our dime dances, our football games, the hours we were kept after school, grumping
through geometry in Mrs. Bunnell's classroom, our whole-
world-is-watching student council campaigns. Nothing will
bring back Ricky Roche's fat-fendered orange roadster or Scott
Reinking's sleek white Thunderbird or Jim Dodd's Cuba Lake
Chris Craft. I speak here of older boys, godlike in their modes
of transportation, who did not see me as they passed. But I
remember them, the older boys: Doug Nicot in his handwoven
jacket of many colors, turning briefly toward me on his stool

in Cretekos and saying, "Skip a couple of birthdays and I'll take you out." His words caused me to slosh my milkshake on the counter in a mix of ecstasy and dread.

Nothing will bring back jumping from my Osborne Street porch into the leaves with George Tate, my first love and boy next door. Nothing will bring back those few weeks in Fall 1962 when Jim McPheters just happened to be driving his car up East Pearl Street each morning and would casually offer me a ride to school. But alas, later that year he was driving up East Pearl Street to pick up Joanie Keough!

Nothing will bring back the hour of dancing with The Lover at our Sophomore class party. I remember it well, what I was wearing even. The dress was very tight at the waist and it was hard to breathe. But breathing was irrelevant while dancing with The Lover. He danced close, real close. "Thanks," I said to The Lover, very cool, when respiration returned at the Coke table, whence he had deposited me before seeking another partner. I reviewed my dance with The Lover the next morning, and I still run it by on occasion — you know, if I'm having a bad day or something.

I'm sorry to be personalizing this great theme, Carpe Diem, the motto for Wellsville High School and for us all. But that's the thing about a great theme. Everyone can possess it by filling in the blanks with their own stuff. I was just giving a demonstration. The boys I didn't kiss are my regrets. We all have them, regrets.

I'm not advocating a mass mid-life crisis. We have the wisdom of our years now, and we know we can't take Carpe Diem all that literally. We don't leave happy homes for wild affairs. We know what love is by now, because we have it, or we have had it and lost it, in which case we hope to have it again. We know the love that people call true in this world is tough and forgiving, at the same time it is fragile and rare. There was a time for kissing boys, but it has passed, the way all things pass. But we can mourn it, can't we?

Our reunion lets us think crazy thoughts of being young in Wellsville, New York, in a far more innocent world. It makes us want to hold a little of that craziness and innocence within us. We look at each other and think: Hey, not so bad! We are still sort of young, only in the middle of our lives, after all. There are changes we can make, trips we can take. There are many moments and days left to seize. We can start by seizing this one. A little later we'll ask The Rogues for a special request for the Class of 1963, that all-time great Carpe Diem hit: "C'mon Baby, Let the Good Times Roll."

THE FAMILY
THAT HAD ME

A Note

As I write this my father's wife may be giving birth to his twelfth child. "Thirteenth," my mother corrects me in a phone conversation. My mother is no longer my father's wife and has not been these twenty years. She lives alone and has taken back her maiden name: Flynn. But when she was his wife she had ten living children by him, and one stillbirth, carried to term, a full nine months. It is understandable that she would speak for this dead baby, want it counted. I once knew, but cannot remember, whether it was my brother or sister.

So that makes eleven children in my father's first family. He had a twelfth by his second wife, who had two children by a previous marriage. And now he is having a thirteenth child by his third wife, who has one child by a previous marriage. You could, I suppose say, that he has been father to sixteen children, and that I should have been a sister to them all.

I am his firstborn. Growing up in a big house in a small town, I had six sisters and three brothers. One of my brothers is dead now, murdered at 29, pursued into the Hudson River where he drowned. My mother's house is beside the Hudson River. She can look out her front window and see its waters in all seasons, its ice floes in winter. She has never remarried. And I live 150 miles from her, in the world's greatest city, formed by this same river.

My father divorced my mother when I was in my early twenties and already married. It was a terrible divorce. We had been raised very strictly in the Catholic faith and this was not something we ever expected to happen to us. I felt very sad for my younger brothers and sisters, who suffered a great deal,

11

but I counted myself lucky. I was an adult, married, with a college education and a secure teaching job. At least, I thought, I would not be affected.

When I was a child, I thought we were such a happy family, so strong and special and large.

The Sock Drawer
(1989)

The sock drawer was a large drawer to the right of our kitchen sink, just below the knives and forks and next to the junk drawer. It was my mother's solution to the laundry. The name was a euphemism, for, although it did house the entire family's abandoned mateless socks, its chief function was to contain the underpants of the female offspring. The drawers drawer, if you will. But we were of Irish descent and reticent in certain areas, and so we called it the sock drawer. Or was the name simply due to the number of syllables in underpants as against socks? (We would never have shortened it to panties! We hated the word panties. It has connotations.)

There were ten children, so to avoid total chaos, my mother liked to have a system when she could. For her laundry system, she set up metal shelving in the cellarway and affixed our names to it with masking tape. She put each child's pile of folded clean clothes above the name. You were responsible for emptying your pile. If you didn't, it got quite high, in inverse proportion to the contents of your bureau. Paul, for example, almost never emptied his pile. "Empty your pile!" my mother would yell at him in frustration. A lost article of clothing would invariably be discovered weeks later at the bottom of an unemptied pile.

The pile system, though flawed, was good for most things, except the underpants. There were seven girls. How was my mother to distinguish among the white cotton Spankies, which differed only in slight gradations of size and rips and strength of elastic? She despaired of separating them into piles and so

13

put all the girls' underpants into the sock drawer. (Boys were different. Their underpants looked different. There were only three boys, two close in age, the other a baby.)

We sisters would come downstairs in the dark mornings of a western New York winter and stand before the sock drawer, chilly and penitent in our nightgowns, or dripping in a towel, waiting for our turn to rummage about. Sometimes you would grab blindly and get the mousetrap or a bunch of rusty wire meant for the junk drawer. Or, if you got up late, and Mom hadn't done a wash in a day or so, you might find only baby Brigid's training pants or the big pink flannel long johns left by Nana on her last visit. You would stand there in the cold dawn and know a truth about yourself, which was that today you would not be too high-and-mighty to wear the long johns.

I have to say it: there was, at times, discord. There were, sometimes, fisticuffs over a particularly good pair.

We have not been girls together for many years. Women now, seared by the sock drawer, we carry its lessons within us. Humility. Competition. Exultation in the homely. The inexorable law of the supply side. We walk through life, women confused about lingerie.

Me, for instance. I linger before the local lingerie boutique, awed by rich satins, ribbons, laces, embroidery, handpainted rosettes on silk, the sheer and sensual variety of bustiers and teddies and camisoles and tap pants. And, sometimes, I duck inside, reasoning that it is better to be in the store than out on the street staring at string bikinis. (You could attract someone weird.)

Lingerie stores intimidate me. They induce guilt. Once inside, I tentatively touch the goods. I look at my hand through the lace. If a salesgirl is watching, I might murmur something lingerie-appropriate, like "how lovely." But I almost never buy, because I am cheap about lingerie. Though I am capable of spending wantonly in other areas, I am, to my sorrow, a generic underwear shopper. The truth is, I feel unworthy!

It was a fit of underwear unworthiness that caused me, years ago, to return my husband's first married gift to me. I put it back in the box and took it to Saks the next day, telling him it was the wrong size. It was the right size (I had tried it on) and it was beautiful, but it was lingerie, an elegant lounging ensemble in a soft yellow. Saks? We had no money then. I exchanged it for something sensible that would show. I do not remember now what it was that was so sensible and would show, but I do remember the gift, which would only have been seen by my young husband, the silky feel of the pants against my legs, how the satin jacket was quilted and had a mandarin-style collar, how proud and happy he had been when he gave it to me.

It is a commonplace conundrum of the social sciences that psyches from the same gene pool can respond very differently to the same stimulus. The sock drawer has given my sister Taine this extreme sense of entitlement about lingerie. She has given herself permission. She goes on lingerie binges. She will tell you: "Anyone who shared our sock drawer deserves to have beautiful underwear!"

Recently I visited a woman who told me a lingerie factory store had just opened in her town. A brand-name lingerie factory store. We went. It had none of the ambiance of my lingerie boutique. The hangers weren't padded. No wafting scent of tea rose. No matter. There was a bounty of gorgeous underthings for a fraction of the retail cost. Racks and racks of the stuff. My mouth went dry. Seized by a panic-buying urge far greater than the ones I've experienced before blizzards and hurricanes, I embraced a bunch of teddies in my size, clutched them to my heart and carried them off in delight to my companion.

"What are you going to do with all of those things?" she asked. She had selected a flannel nightgown and was heading for the cashier.

I shrugged. I blushed. I stood there dumbfounded. Though we had never talked teddy before, this woman and I, I knew that she knew what they're for. I stammered, "Uh...I don't know...I might not get back here for a while. I thought I'd buy a few and they'd last me."

"You got so many they'll last forever. You'll still be wearing them when the crotch is hanging down around your knees."

What did she mean? I believe she meant it as a metaphor, some kind of trenchant comment on my overweening vanity and certain mortality. Or was it a joke? I laughed weakly and bought them anyway, but with less delight. The woman's identity is not relevant, since she was not herself at that moment. I believe, truly, that she had been invaded by body snatchers and was serving as a mere medium for a far greater power, the stern spirit of the sock drawer past.

Reaching for My Brother
(1985)

The Vietnam veterans' parade, May 7, 1985: I saw my generation pass in review, a fair chunk of it anyway, wearing jungle fatigues in the canyon of Lower Manhattan. It didn't look so good. I look better. Younger, less lined about the face. Slimmer, though some I saw were very slim indeed. Less fright in the eye area. Fewer scars.

There's a reason. I'm a woman. These are men.

They look as if they've been through a war.

My daughter sings a song now, a joyful, rope-jumping, hand-clapping song that stops me cold:

"My father went to war war war
In nineteen sixty-four four four
He brought me back a gun gun gun
And the gun...went...BANG!"

Her father didn't go to war because he joined the Reserves in '64, before the escalation. Her uncle went, though. Her uncle, my brother, went to Vietnam on an aircraft carrier. His body looked about the same when he came home as when he left, but they paid him full disability anyway. And he didn't die by land mine but by Hudson River water, and then not until four years after Saigon fell. My brother who swam strong in lake water when he was three years old.

★　★　★

Death by drowning, they said. My brother was murdered, pursued by a band of thugs from a bar, across I-787, until he

17

tried to escape them by plunging down a fifteen-foot embankment into the Hudson. They found his body three days later. You know what you know. He would never have been so weakened before Vietnam.

I know about destroyed men. So, apparently, does this woman next to me. She's black, neatly coifed, wearing a spring silk dress on this day of changing weather. I figure she works in the area. And me, I'm white, her age, in dungarees and greasy hair, here after dropping my kid off at school. We would make a good picture, this woman and I. The caption would be "Women Grieve." People around us are laughing and waving little American flags. We don't speak or offer each other tissues. Neither of us has any. It's a little embarrassing. We just weep.

The crown applauds most for the ones without legs. I have a hard time applauding them since I know I've walked by some of them on the street before. Revered today, reviled tomorrow and yesterday. C'est la vie. C'est la guerre.

I was one of Spiro Agnew's effete snobs. The brass buckle on my belt was a peace sign. I made black armbands for the Moratorium and handed them out on 14th Street. I marched on Washington a few times. We marched past Nixon's inauguration to the Washington Monument and Peter, Paul and Mary: "And if you take my hand, my son, all will be well when the day is done." I caught whiffs of tear gas and drank from someone's flask on the train going back to New York.

I am waving like a fool to these men as they pass, and they are waving back to me, but I want to rasie my hand in a V sign. Declare a truce between us. The thing is, I don't dare. They don't know me. But I'm hardly the only one at this parade under wraps, crying in camouflage.

I could not stay away.

My brother sent a letter home. "I put everybody's name on bombs," it said. He wrote it when he was young, and I read it when I was young. I read it now with older eyes. "Have fun at Lake George," he wrote.

Even if I had been a man, I would certainly have got a deferment. I was pre-lottery; so was my brother. I was a good student; he wasn't. I went to college. He dropped out of high school and enlisted in the Navy before they could draft him.

A wisp of a middle-aged man in a dirty red T-shirt falls out of rank and approaches us on the sidelines. He leans on the police barricade, and, choked with booze, tears, emotion tongue can't tell, repeats, "I love it. . . . I love it," his arms outstretched, taking in all of Broadway, the bagpipes plainting "America the Beautiful," the falling bombs of shredded paper, and all of us. Then he passes on. "A druggie," a boy near me says to his girl, and they titter. It may be true, but it seems a mean-spirited, smug summation — here, today. I feel like grabbing their young heads by their lustrous hair and shaking them a little, just until they get things straight.

"My immediate future is undecided," my brother wrote me when he returned to the States. It was to include stays at the Palo Alto V.A. and the Albany V.A.

A huge man in woolly beard and red bandanna passes, then backs up to plant a slobbering, unsolicited kiss on the pretty policewoman in front of me. His buddies laugh, but she is shaken. I use this incident, or try to, to get a grip. I wouldn't like all of these guys. I probably wouldn't like a lot of them. It's no matter. Here, today.

Some look O.K. They look as if they've eschewed junk for jogging. They look as though they've made their way. I am grateful that they've left their jobs today to march with these others. Why should I be? There's certainly not a trace of condescension in their step. They were probably officers then, too, these well-kept men, or did any of them actually work their

way up through the ranks from grunt green to Barneys Madison
Room civvies?

It keeps on keeping on. Electrical Worker Vets, Transit Cop
Vets, vets in greenface, vets wearing orange Agent Orange armbands, Gay Vets, Black Vets for Social Justice, California Vets,
a tall stunned vet with thinning blond hair, walking with his
aging mother.

A high-school rifle squad, in purple and white twitchy skirts,
twirls white wood rifles. The Victory in Vietnam Committee
passes, carrying its banner, "America Is Number One, Thanks
to Our Vets." A guy goes by carrying a baby in pink, and I
am inordinately happy for his ordinary life. But then, three
men pass walking with three perfect little sons, but these sons
are wearing *little fatigues*. Some folks learn their lessons real
hard.

★   ★   ★

It started on the IRT on my way to the parade. I grabbed
on to the same pole as a man my height and age. He had fine
tracings of red in his white, puffy skin. His nose was broken,
an old break, but there was a new scab across the broken
bridge. There were scabs on the hand that held the pole, too,
and on the one that grasped the cracked molded briefcase, and
dirt under ragged nails. He had a thick blond mustache, bushy
sideburns and red-rimmed eyes. His hair was carefully parted
and combed down. The collar of his brown striped shirt was
loose and limp. His tie was too wide and so were his lapels.
Traces of grime were evident on the raised weave of his pale
synthetic suit. It was years old, that suit. Years out of style.
It might have been his job-hunting suit when he first came back.

He saw me and smiled tentatively, but then not at all. Our
eyes kept meeting. He knew me and I knew him. We were going

to the same place. I wanted to move my hand down until it touched his. I wanted to lean against the pole and reach for him and hold my brother.

A Child's Christmas
in Wellsville
(1987)

This is my heartwarming Christmas essay, which was also heart-felt. But, because it was written on commission to be heartwarm-ing, it does not show both the yin and the yang, the holly and the humbug, of my Christmas neurosis. I have a dark Yuleside that I wish to recognize in this, my book: I know what Christmas does to women. Traditions are built on the backs of women. Men have a walk-on part for the holidays. They make a cameo appearance. They leave the brandied cheeseball and the TV to walk to the table and carve the bird. Their magazines do not exhort them to start making cookies weeks early, so as not to be mortified, caught short when friends drop by. One recent Christmas, Saks even considerately set up two TV's on the sixth floor "so that Dad can watch his favorite football game while the rest of the family shops." I know of a woman with three small children who suffered a nervous breakdown at Christmas. "She had to go and do it now," her husband said. As though she had a choice; as though Christmas weren't a perfectly sensible time.

The family was everything to us when we lived in Wellsville, and Christmas was the family. By family I mean our immediate family, which came to include ten children and our smiling, pied Brownie, she of the doubtful pedigree and enthusiastic bark. Wellsville is a very small town, and cold and white in winter. It is in a remote corner of New York State, a whole night train's ride away from New York City and all of my

mother's relatives. Which was why we didn't go there, though
I know my mother longed for her family at Christmas, for New
York City at Christmas. She was still a girl and a war was
ending when she married my father in the city. She married
him on the day after Christmas, when the altar was banked
with poinsettias.

"Who would want us, anyway?" my mother would say, "so
many kids." It hurt my feelings when she said that, to think
that people wouldn't want to see me and my younger brothers
and sisters, especially at Christmas when my mother worked
very hard to make us all look so nice. I, for instance, would
get to wear my red taffeta dress with its own crinoline and
its wide lace collar. Paulie and Kevin could wear their short-
pants, no-collar navy wool suits. I thought we were a wonderful family and that anyone would want us, be delighted to host
us for however long we wanted to stay. Our relatives certainly
wanted us, didn't they?

And though Wellsville was my father's hometown, his
parents and all his brothers had moved away. The only relatives
we had there were Teresa and Dorothy, maiden sisters, cousins
to my grandmother. My mother made a lot of them, though
they were much older, only remotely related to my father, and
no kin to her at all.

Teresa and Dorothy would always make a visit in the week
before Christmas, and they would always arrive at bedtime.
While they were still standing in our doorway, stamping snow
off their fur-trimmed, high-heeled boots, removing the
accordion-pleated plastic that protected their blue-ish marcelled
hair, Paulie would hear them, or maybe Susan. *"Teresa and
Dorothy are here!"* someone would shout, and we bounded
heedless down the stairs, in ripped pajamas, in a towel maybe,
hair still soapy and unrinsed, a runny-nosed laughing baby
bringing up the rear in just an undershirt. Teresa and Dorothy

would delightedly scoop us up and hug us to them, grazing our cheeks slightly with the holly and snowman corsages that were pinned to the shawl collars of their pastel wool coats.

"What did you bring us?" a little kid, Peggy or Mary Ann would demand, but we big kids knew. It was the gift they always brought us at Christmas: a large, pine-sprigged tin of that ethereal cocktail mix made from Cheerios, peanuts, and Rice and Wheat Chex, still warm and greasy from their skillet. *"Teresa and Dorothy are here!"* My mother ushered her guests into her living room, made a fire, poured brandy, and rolled red wax back on a Gouda. (My father would not be there. He was a doctor and was often out making calls.) The kind ladies exclaimed over the creche, the tree, and oh, so many Christmas cards!

We, meanwhile, assembled on the floor around the coffee table and pounced upon that tin of terrific stuff. While we ate and anxiously watched how many times each fist went into the tin, the big kids were obliged to tell Teresa and Dorothy how school was and which nun we had that year. We had to look away from the tin and at Dorothy when we spoke to her, taking care to move our lips, because Dorothy was profoundly deaf. What we did, actually, was shout at her.

But I digress. The cocktail mix: I preferred the Chex, for its property of grafting on to the salt and melted butter. Paul liked the Cheerios and Kevin the peanuts. Susan liked it all. It was gone in a moment, and then we would run our fingers over the tin for the crumbs.

When Teresa and Dorothy left, it was us again, the family, alone with Christmas. But we children didn't know that, that we were alone, bound together in a small snowy town. We had our parents and we had each other. We had the Church and Midnight Mass and the school's Christmas pageant. Mainly what we had was our mother, who taped Christmas cards over the archway, looped boughs through our banister, sewed satin and tinsel to coathanger angel wings, and suffered us to decorate countless cookies.

I am older now than my parents were then, and when I think of the family, of wanting to be with the family at Christmas, I think of my mother. She was with us, her new family, but it wasn't her first family — it wasn't her mother and the leg of lamb she made; it wasn't her lovely tall sisters who now had families of their own. As she showed Taine Marie and Che-che how to glue paper together to make a red chain for the tree, did she ever look up and wonder who they were, all these children, and this man she lived with now?

I am far from Wellsville and the people I loved then, the things I believed in then. I have small Christmases now with my small family. And though I love this family, it's this other family I yearn for at Christmas. But that family is gone now, away from Wellsville and each other. We will never be all together again. My parents are long divorced. My brother Paul is dead. Others are far away: Texas, California, Washington. There are many reasons why we can't be home. It is enough to say distance.

And so we try to make family of those we are near, our friends and neighbors, the way my mother did with Teresa and Dorothy in 1958.

Portrait Fear
(1988)

My walls are lined with pictures. One, from sixty years ago,
shows my mother's family, posed in front of what seem to be
the Baths of Caracalla, but it was really Astoria. Or maybe
Kate and Bill Flynn dressed their seven children and made the
journey into "the City" for the day. It was taken in a studio,
for the Flynn household would not have had those scrolled
mahogany armchairs. My teenage aunts sport flapper dresses
and bobs with marcels. Uncle Bill, hair slick and thick, has
clearly outgrown his jacket. Johnny, retired now from the
NYPD, radiates sweetness in his sailor suit. And my mother,
age three, in ringlets, with smocking on her dress and
foreboding on her face forever, will always be clutching my
grandmother's chair.

Next to that one is an oval, Kate's greenhorn picture — what
she called it and what it was. You got off the boat, you got
a job and a room, and then you went to a portrait studio for
evidence to send to the old country of your prosperity in the
new.

Kate, at nineteen, was a cook for a Park Avenue family. She
certainly borrowed the gold watch, the pin, and the locket she
wore...studio props, perhaps, along with the paper roses in
the vase beside her.

Then there are the Christmas-card portraits of my siblings
and me. Every year the photographer arrived in November.
Every year a new kid and a new gimmick. There we are,
crowding onto the coffee table that had been shoved in front
of the fireplace. One year we're faking a ski scene; the next,

smiling from the tree house or packing into the van we finally got. The year Mary Ann had the mumps her school picture was superimposed on our portrait, with an arrow pointing to "Mumps." Mary Ann was not amused.

The latest addition is the family portrait my brother sent each of us. Boy, did Kevin get credit for it — my father mentioned it in his Christmas letter while neglecting to note the rest of us. As I look at it, I wonder what caused my rough-hewn carpenter brother and his wife to dress up and drive the fifty miles from Pahrump, Nev., to the Olan Mills Portrait Studio in Las Vegas, trying to keep their little boys neat all that way. They succeeded. The only thing Jim got on his rugby shirt was a little laugh drool.

These pictures rated the wall because they've been done. A decision was made; time and effort and at least a little money were needed to get them, and so respect must be afforded them. It is why the portrait of the Flynn family of 1928 has come to me, while snapshots are lost or languish in forgotten albums. And once a picture makes the wall, it's always there — an unconscious presence of love and loss.

What slugs! We have no formal portrait of my daughter or of the three of us together. Have we no sense of history, do we think ourselves unworthy, or are we just lazy asses? Don't we love our kid enough? Can her yearly one-shot-per-kid, mottled-background school pictures be enough? Doesn't the flash on my camera make her blue eyes red? Why have a portrait when video captures her moves and voice? But will VHS recorders always be with us? Besides, it takes real commitment to find the tape, stick it in, and sit through last year's Halloween party or her earnest interpretation of *all* of "The Greatest Love of All." But a picture on the wall is with you when you're doing taxes.

Or are we afraid? For, if we do it, if we actually go someplace, the three of us, and pose together, what will become of our portrait? Can we hope that it will find its way to the wall of a loving grandchild sixty years hence?

Some Write Songs,
Some Deliver the Mail
(1985)

When my sister Mary Ann was nineteen she changed her
name to Ruby. Just Ruby, not Ruby Rockwell, not Ruby
anything. While she was Ruby she wore thirties dresses and
a lot of makeup and she sang us songs the way Janis sang them.
"Get it while you can," she sang to us one summer's end on
an old screened porch in the night, in the rain that came
through to us a little from the roof we had neglected. We sat
quiet, wrapped in blankets drinking beer and listening to Ruby,
and in the light from the kerosene lamp, we saw how her pretty
young face grew dark in the singing.

It's years since we called her Ruby. She's been married and
divorced; she has a child now, and a life 3,000 miles from mine.
She's Mary Ann again, but Ruby lives in her and permits her
to do brave and inconvenient things.

★ ★ ★

Lately what she did was quit the P.O., where she has worked
for four years, first as a clerk and then as a mail carrier. She
quit because her supervisors timed her when she went to the
bathroom and stood behind her as she cased her mail. She
quit because she didn't like ten-hour days. She quit because,
after she got bitten by the dog, a supervisor filing the report
said that waving her coat may have provoked the dog. My
sister is no provoker of dogs. She waved her coat after the fact,

in a frantic attempt to unsic the dog from her leg. She quit because she was tired of being assigned new routes each day. She quit because mail carriers, expecially the female ones, are expected to smile and chat with everyone along the route, and are met with hostility when they don't, because they can't, because they have no time. She quit because the exponential increase in the amount of junk mail made it nearly impossible to take a lunch hour. She quit, in sum, because she hated it.

People counseled her against quitting in the strongest possible terms. You're a single mother with a young child. It pays $11 an hour, terrific for someone without a degree. You have medical benefits. You can transfer to some other city if you don't like it there. You already have four years in — in twenty-one more years you can retire.

She called me. "If you hate it, quit it," I told her in a very small voice.

"Thank you, thank you," she said. "At last someone tells me it's O.K. to quit something that I hate!"

I didn't want to tell her to quit either. I wanted to remind her of her perilous non-degreed-single-mother status. I wanted to lecture her, tell her we were talking a job with the Government, hear? — not your five-and-dime or waitress job. Weren't people supposed to be grateful for Government jobs? I sincerely wished there were some way the P.O. and Mary Ann could come to terms.

I knew Mary Ann wanted to quit and it scared me. I didn't want to think of my younger sister in another corner of the country, starting over in a life that has not been easy. I would feel responsible if things didn't work, though I know that Mary Ann certainly didn't hold me or anyone else responsible. It would have been easier for everyone concerned if she had stayed in her place. For everyone but Mary Ann and her child.

Concerned everyones can be a problem.

Do not change, says their siren song. *Do not change. We love you the way you are. We may not love the new you.*

Please, please, you chorus. *Let me change.* Until one day you act without permission, or you do not act.

Usually change doesn't bring giddy success or dismal failure. Nothing so scary as either of these. And it doesn't happen all at once. Allen Ginsberg's psychiatrist took a casual approach when he gave him this advice on whether to leave his job to write poetry: "Don't worry about it now. You're an interesting guy." I like it. It's relaxed, generous, hopeful. I see Allen Ginsberg sometimes in our neighborhood diner. He looks like he's doing O.K.

★ ★ ★

My sister is still struggling, but not under the weight of hundreds of sample boxes of Glisso addressed to "Occupant." She has enrolled in a culinary arts program with the intent of opening her own catering business one day. She left her apartment to share a house with another single mother, dividing rent, child care, and responsibilities. She's living on a student loan and a waitressing job. Instead of singing for her supper, she cooks meals for her singing teacher to pay for her voice lessons.

For a time, the chopping motion required in her apprenticeship as a prep chef caused tendinitis in her arm and a fear that she might not be able to continue in the culinary arts. Ironically it was her right arm, so well developed from hauling mailbags, that showed this weakness. While her arm was mending, she and her child came across country for a visit. "Sit," I told her as I made her a drink. "Someone should take care of you for a while." My saying this made her cry.

She had a kind of guilt about quitting because she was a woman in a nontraditional job. Should she have stayed to make a point? When she first started at the post office, she met Edith, a woman in her mid-forties with thick chestnut hair who gave as good as she got, trading raunchy insults with the male carriers. She'd been there for years, one of the first women to carry mail in the country. She'd endured assignments foisted upon no man, such as years of night collections in the inner city. "We're trying to make you quit," her bosses told her outright. Mary Ann saw her as a kind of model and congratulated her on being a pioneer, on sticking it out.

Edith nodded and smiled. "But I wish I had quit," she said. "I might have had a good job by now."

★   ★   ★

Mary Ann wants to be a chef. She wants to write songs and sing them, the way Ruby sang them. She loves to dance. When she was thirteen, she wrote a poem and her English teacher sent it off to a national magazine, which bought it, just like that, the first time out. My sister is an artist.

But lots of artists languish in the workplace. There aren't enough jobs out there for all the bright people who want creative, rewarding work. And sadly, the boring jobs need to get done too. But they will not get done by Mary Ann, because she has decided not to do them.

She says she still breaks out in a cold sweat when she thinks of the future, but she is also given to moments of exuberance. There are few occasions in life as exhilarating as quitting a job you hate. One of the all-time great song titles has to be "Take This Job and Shove It." We sing about leaving good jobs in the city, not working on Maggie's farm no more, and the sadness of souls owed to the company store. I can hear Ruby belting one of them out.

Kate's Death in America
(1986)

There is only one loss, they say. The first loss. All other losses
are the first one again, because you know. For me it was the
death of my grandmother — Catherine Flynn, Kate, Katie
Kirby that was — the person who loved me most purely, the
only one to ever call me "Kathleen Mavourneen." Her notes
with crumpled fives or tens followed me wherever I went. "To
my lovely girl," they would always say, and always be signed,
"Lovingly, Nana XOXOXO."

She came to New York City in 1907. She was nineteen with
a fourth-grade education and $40 in her pocket. She came from
a thatched cottage, where the dog would know the donkey
was coming when the donkey was still miles down the road.
Her sister Maggie was here already. Brothers — Nick, Jack,
and Dan — came before her and after her. Bartholomew died
young. Tom stayed behind in Limerick.

Kate went to work on Park Avenue as a cook for a doctor
whose son Charley was forever coming to her to borrow a few
bucks. Charley was no dope.

Maggie died and left four children, one of them an infant
six weeks old. Though she had so recently given birth, Maggie
insisted on attending a friend's funeral, right to the grave. It
was a damp, fall day. She was dead the next day. Spinal
meningitis, though her husband said she caught her death of
cold at the gravesite. There was only one course for Kate. She
left her job and went with her brother Nick to live in her sister's
house to raise the children.

After a few years she married her sister's husband and had children of her own. She married Bill Flynn, who had a great temper and made poteen from potato mash in a copper still in the cellar. But also in the cellar were cobbler's tools to mend his children's shoes. Bill was very handsome and a good provider to boot. "He was never out of work a day, not even during the Depression." That's what they said about Bill Flynn. He worked and saved and became the landlord for a six-family apartment house.

He also bought a house for his own family in Astoria and a plot of land beside it for the chickens and the goat. Kate would milk the goat and playfully squeeze a teat at any child that came near. My mother remembers the goat milk, warm and sweet, on her face, on her tongue. A man, he was Jewish, stopped one day as my grandmother was milking and asked to buy a cup. He had tuberculosis, he said, and goat's milk would be good for him. She gave him goat's milk every day thereafter. She strained the hairs out first in a very fine sieve. She would not hear of payment.

Kate had her children at home, delivered by Dr. Amato. My mother was six when her infant sister was brought to her in the kitchen. "Can we keep it?" she asked.

"When I was your age, I could jump over the rooftops," Kate would tell my mother. She said she would go to the dances and dance all night. Everyone wanted to dance with her, because she was such a good dancer. She believed in the little people and in Nick Brown, who, back in her town, had the power to put off bad marriages. She invoked Nick Brown's spirit if she worried that her granddaughters were taking up with unworthy young men. "Marry a kind man," she told me. I took her advice.

She knew how to take care of men who were kind, men like my husband who played the harmonica in her living room. "Get him another beer," she'd order me.

"He can get his own beer, Nana." My husband would remove the harmonica from his mouth and grin broadly. It was a scene that had been played out before. A scene he cherished.

"Ah, well then... I'll get it for him meself," she'd say, and begin to struggle with the arms of her chair in an effort to pull her weight up. Her poor old hands would tremble a bit as she reached for her cane. My husband would remain seated, serene.

"Damn it, I'll get it!" I would flash them both my fury and stalk out to the refrigerator as they, in the living room, exchanged a conspiratorial smile.

She could be tough, but to her children, never to her children's children. "The back of me hand to you," she told her children often, and sometimes followed through.

Her philosophy was "Come merry, come sorry," or its variation, "Never a fine day came, but a rainy day came after." She knew... being Irish, having lived. I have had many a fine day now, but as I live each one, I hear her caution.

She went back to Ireland once for a visit after years, after a life, and she saw her brother Tom. "Are you Kate?" he asked her. "Was your mother my mother?"

She died as people do these days, especially when they have lived to be old: in a major hospital center, one with the technology that she had never known, on tubes, on a respirator. She could not talk because the respirator was in her mouth. She could not see well. She could not sit up. Her arms were tied to the bed as a safeguard.

I went to see her on Christmas Day. A priest came by and gave her a turtle made from a walnut shell by someone in a nursing home. He had a trayful of turtles.

I have the notes she scrawled on the pad I steadied on the edge of her mattress for her as I listened to the relentless squashing sound of false breathing. I saved them because they were her last words to me, barely legible because she was old, because she could not lift her head to see as she wrote, because her arm was tied and she could only move it close at her side. A few words only on each small page:

"are you"

"take me home"

"drink water"

"I want sit up"

"they cant keep me here"

"are you Kathy?"

THE FAMILY I HAD

What's a Bum, Mom?
(1985)

"That one is a bum. That one is a drug addict." Isabelle, at five, has a firm grip on verities that have eluded me these last few years. I am walking her and my daughter through the five blocks of sidewalk from kindergarten to ballet class. Isabelle is our guide. We've walked around three men lying asleep on the sidewalk, stepping over a streak of urine that has made its way from one man to the curb. ("Are they asleep? Are they sick? Are they dead? What's the matter with them?" my daughter asks. "They're bums," Isabelle explains.) We've declined to give money to a woman who has asked us for 25 cents. I excuse myself to myself by saying that my hands are full with the children's hands.

"Why does she want 25 cents, Mom? Can't she get 25 cents herself? Why didn't you give her 25 cents if she needs money?"

"We're late for ballet," I say. How can I stop now to rummage in my pockets for quarters? And what if I don't have a quarter? I'm getting real good at excuses.

"Thank you," says the woman. "God bless you."

★　★　★

We wait for the light at 14th. Opposite us, a man wearing ripped high tops and a sheer slip is also waiting. His beard is matted filth and his head is bandaged. He is shouting and gesticulating. I feel baby hands tighten on mine. Their bodies lean against my legs. As he passes us in the crosswalk he lurches toward us. The girls grab my arms and scream. "Yuk," says

Isabelle, when we are safely past. "That one stinks!" He does, and the stench of him fouls even the air he has gone from.

"What is a bum, Mom? I mean, how do you know?" my daughter asks that night. She needs an explanation for the people that she sees on the streets. She has to know why. She has to find out about human misery. It is all around her.

"I'm taking you to the Precinct," a man tells me the next afternoon as I'm walking my daughter home. "You ragged five dollars off me."

"Walk fast," I tell my daughter, but I didn't have to. I figure once we're past, he'll go to the next passer-by. But he doesn't. His deranged mind has singled me out. He grabs my arm as I turn to go into my building. My terrified daughter is hanging onto my other arm. Just then my neighbor Shelley comes out of our building with her three-year-old daughter. I want her to go back in, but she is too good a friend, and too brave.

"Sir, you leave her alone! I'm going to call the police."

"I'm taking her to the Precinct. She ragged five dollars off me."

"She didn't rag five dollars off anyone, sir!"

I should scream, but I cannot. Though my reflexes have worked in other emergencies, having my daughter as a hostage in this one has rendered me immobile. I am mute, thinking dumbly, as if at the distance I wish I were:

Shelley is my good, good friend.

I should have gone to the Precinct.

Shelley is calling him "sir."

Shelley knew right away what "ragged" meant.

Does he have a knife?

His face is menacing, filled with hatred. I know he is going to hurt me, but I am frozen, listening to my daughter, who is screaming, crying.

A large man in a sweatshirt comes from somewhere and pulls him from me, but he grabs me again. The large man has to hit him, actually deck him in front of our little daughters, before we can escape.

"He thought you took his five dollars, Mom? Did somebody really take his five dollars? Why didn't you give him five dollars and he would go away? He's in jail now, right? How long will they keep him in jail? Until he knows not to hurt somebody?"

I have another story, of another mother and her teen-age daughter who live on the ground floor of a lovely old building in the West Village. There is a moatlike depression in the front of the building. A homeless man built a house for himself in the moat, from discarded plywood. The house the man built was right outside the daughter's window. She heard him in the night the way my daugher hears her hamster. In the morning he was gone, and she and her mother dismantled his house. In the afternoon, when they returned home, they found his house rebuilt. That evening he threw a rock through their front window.

I take after my daughter. I've got a lot of questions. Why were these women forced into this situation? What is it like, taking down a man's house before the winter? They had to do it, anyone would have done it, but did they cry while they were doing it?

Why are thousands of people without homes in this city? Why are deranged people on the streets where they will harm or be harmed? Why have they not been given the dignity of a place?

I've lived too long and seen too much for Isabelle's answers. A woman defecating in the waiting room at Penn Station. A man, clearly sick and in pain, ushered between two security guards from the place in front of their building where he had been lying, to a sidewalk across the street. Bouncers at the doors

of our libraries keeping them out. A supermarket manager
bodily removing a man who came in to redeem a few scavenged
deposit bottles.

From a bus window I saw a woman with oozing ankles shuffle
in pain and pieces of shoes as she carried her bags. She stopped
at a wastebasket and retrieved a large discarded sketch book.
She flipped through it until she found a blank page. Standing
on the corner of Sixth and 14th, she reached into one of her
bags and found a marker. She made one deft stroke, then
another, on the page another artist left her. My bus moved on.

★   ★   ★

I can no longer say *bum* or *bag lady*. And, that most invidious
term *street people*, with its implication that the street is where
they are happiest, doing their thing, merrily rifling for rotted
food in the supermarket garbage bins, gladly searching out a
place to wash their bodies. So I tell my daughter that they are
homeless and try to explain what that means. I try to explain
why. Some of them can't think right. Some of them can hurt
people. All of them are hungry. I do not tell her that there
are children among them. I do not tell her that many of these
people are sick and some are dying from hunger and exposure
and neglect.

I have plenty more questions than I have answers. I've always
been good at putting questions to others. It's right: there's need
here, there's agony, there's blame. But now I have a daughter
who demands answers from me and *will* get them. She observes
her mother far too closely. The only true response for her is
the one she sees me make to those whose anguished lives are
being lived so close to hers.

It's My Kid,
She Thinks She's Jewish
(1983)

I had an epiphany at the St. Patrick's Day parade in 1984—
a brisk sparkling Saturday, the sun lavishing gold over all that
green. I was on 86th Street with my daughter, who was at the
time four years old. We were watching the last of the parade.
The day and the shot of Jameson's I had just tossed back, back
at my friend Eileen's, had raised my dormant Irish Catholic
consciousness to a level unmatched since I was seventeen.

The counties were marching by. Clare. Cork. Mayo. Officer
Lenahan and a striped sawhorse marked *Police* keep us from
the parade and the parade from us. This Officer Lenahan is
so cute and merry that I have a crazy urge to buy a "Kiss Me,
I'm Irish" button. I suppress it and instead purchase a green
plastic lei for my daughter.

Just then the kilts and the banners and pipes of County
Limerick march past us. Limerick, where, in the town of
Templeglantin lies a pile of rocks, the foundation only, of a
thatched cottage, my grandmother's first home. The pipes are
really calling me now.

★　　★　　★

"Will you arrest us if we march?" I ask Officer Lenahan.

"I'll arrest you if I see you," is his reply, his mouth smiling
right along with his Irish eyes. In another shot I pull my
daughter under the sawhorse and we join Limerick, delighted

43

to be there at the end of the parade, marching with the counties. Falling into step I squeeze her hand and think of parades past: my family coming into Grand Central from upstate, my mother giving the thumbs-up salute to the marchers, standing for hours unmindful of the cold, corned beef and cabbage after at Horn & Hardart's before the train home.

My daughter pulls at my hand as we walk past Gimbels East. I hardly notice because I'm busy with the other hand, waving to my new public on the curb. She tugs again. She has something to say. I lean toward her, still marching in time to "Garry Owen." Her lei scratches my cheek.

"What is it?" I ask her.

"I guess we're not celebrating Shabbat today, huh, Mom?" says she.

She's confused, my daughter.

She thinks she's Jewish.

She might as well be, is what I realize.

My husband and I come from Catholic backgrounds: Stations of the Cross, meatless Fridays, Lenten sacrifices, altar boy (him) and Sodality of the Virgin Mary (me), Confraternity of Christian Doctrine, Catholic colleges and wedding in the Church of the Sacred Heart.

So how come our daughter thinks she's Jewish? How come, when she was three, she composed her own Christmas carol:

"Santa Claus, O Santa Claus,
Come light the menorah."

It is our own doing. We, the fallen-away Catholics, sought the nearest way. We sent her to nursery school at the Y.M.H.A. A not-bad nursery school. Good as most. It had what we wanted, the main criterion in our choice of school: it was on the corner. We could drop her off and be on the crosstown bus by 8:30. Proximity means a lot when you're dragging a toddler, her lunchbox, Grandpa Smurf, and your briefcase.

"There will of course be some instruction in Jewish culture," the director told us when we signed on, and paused for our reaction.

"Of course," we said. "What's the tuition?"

My friend, the fallen-away Jew, was amazed. "I could never send my kid to a Jewish school." Well sure. We would have had a hard time sending our daughter to a Catholic school, even if it were in the basement of our building. Even if they gave her a full scholarship and came upstairs to get her while we took an extra minute with the newspaper. It's in the nature of being fallen away. You can't go home again, and you don't send your kids.

Italian children and WASP children and a child from Namibia also went to the Y with her. About half of the children were Jewish. But why did my daughter raise her hand when the teacher asked who was Jewish?

She insisted on buying a menorah. After I paid the bill she said, "You don't *have* to buy a menorah — not if you don't celebrate." She, though, was clearly on the side of the celebrants.

She's a serious student. I was too. She pays attention. So did I. I was the only one who *had* to go to daily mass when weekly would have sufficed. And, to my everlasting regret, the only one who obeyed the nuns and didn't make out with boys at high-school parties. Religion is not for the likes of us. We take it too much to heart.

When I was a kid I was surprised to hear that the Jews thought they were chosen, when all along I was. Because I was serious, I used to worry for them, not being baptized and all — and now here's this daughter of mine.

Will she continue to feel Jewish? No. Religion is not like riding a bike. You forget it unless you keep at it. And now she has graduated to kindergarten at the local public school, where, for the time being, the church is separate from the state.

But I wonder, sometimes, whether I am depriving her of something, a richness of culture or a comfort of myth. The pipes will never call her the way they do me. She'll probably never get choked up at hearing "Adeste Fideles" at Christmas. She won't have memories of May Crownings, incensed evenings of new blossoms, pastel organdy dresses, and candle glow — and, in the dark of church, voices chanting the Virgin's Litany, all the beautiful names for Mary, and after each one, "Ora Pro Nobis." But a lot of my emotion at these moments comes from the knowledge that it is a past lost to me, an innocence I can no longer share with people that I love.

She'll have some of it, though, because of the family around her. And I like to think that, growing up on the lower East Side with Baptists and Hindus, Hispanics, blacks, and Pakistanis, she'll share in a true religion of the world. (If I confuse religion and race, it's because they confuse me.)

A Rastafarian with a pride of dreadlocks tells her to finish her Egg McMuffin. A friend's parents make and sell the best cannolis in town. Korean friends own a nearby deli and give her treats each time we buy milk. The Greek florist hands her a daisy and tells me how his children grow tall back in his country. She will have a heritage.

★   ★   ★

At Passover she presents me with an intricate crafting of cardboard. "It's to hold matzoh," she says proudly, and sings a Passover song:
One morning Pharaoh woke in bed
There were frogs on his nose and frogs on his head,
Frogs here, frogs there, frogs were jumping everywhere.
Of Pharaoh, Pharaoh, please let my people go.

At Purim she emerges from class dressed as Queen Esther, with a construction paper crown, a white apron trimmed with pink rickrack. I've answered to "Ima," her father to "Aba." Why not? We're good sports.

At Hanukkah we sing "Spin, Little Dreidel" and she whirls around the room, laughing. When she catches her breath, she begins a march:

"Get a sword and march along with me. Everybody can be a Maccabee."

Which I believe to be the point. Everyone can. A Maccabee or a Catholic or a Moslem. Or whatever else they're taught.

Smack Upside Oedipus
(1984)

A family portrait drawn by the child of the family is the standard icebreaker at parent-teacher conferences in the early grades. Parents are charmed by the drawings and well disposed to the conference that follows. Our nursery-school family portrait was charming. Our daughter had taken pains to provide us with bellybuttons at the same time she cavalierly disposed of other parts of our anatomy: necks, arms, torsos. I was further charmed when the nursery-school teacher pointed out that the figures were in good proportion. The child in the portrait was smaller than the parents, but not so small as to show a poor self-image. The parents were about the same size, which showed that they were both on the scene and equally important to the child. For contrast, the teacher showed me a family portrait by another child — a large mother and child on the front of the page, and Dad relegated to a spot on the back. The teacher and I shared a chuckle over this. I left, congratulating myself on my well-proportioned family and pitying the man on the back of his child's page.

★ ★ ★

This was, as I say, in nursery school. My daughter was three years old. Now she's five. It's Open School night in the kindergarten.

Right away the teacher takes me for a viewing of the family portrait on the door of my daughter's cubby. I know already that the family portrait tells the truth. I am confident, though,

48

as I approach the cubby, and ready now to share a chuckle with the kindergarten teacher. I am not prepred for what I see. The child in question is triumphant. She looks like the "Birth of Venus" if Botticelli had done it when he was five and his medium was Magic Marker. All that hair. Curls and tendrils taking up half the paper. (In real life my daughter does have beautiful curls, which in the summer are streaked golden by the sun. But never so long and glorious as in her art.)

The father, too, is looking good. As tall as the daughter and snappy in bright red pants. His arms are open wide and generous, and he is smiling.

In the lower right-hand corner there is a toadlike figure, a female toad, with medium-length brown hair matted to her head. A toad that could be stomped out by either of the giants in a trifling. I stare at it in disbelief. Face-to-face, smack upside Oedipus.

I like to be cool. It's kind of a code with me. But I lose it in front of this teacher whom I have seen exactly three times before. "Is that me?" I keen. "Is that supposed to be me?" I frantically search the doors of other cubbies for families as warped as mine. I find none, but I haven't checked them all because the teacher is leading me away to a little person's seat. At least the kid got the hair right, I think miserably.

"Is that what it is, the Oedipus complex?" I ask the teacher. "That's what it is, right?" I want a syndrome to file this away in so I'm not a bad mother. It's important that this teacher know I'm not a bad mother. It has to be a syndrome, and she has to know I know it. The teacher doesn't seem to give much weight to this and rightly wants to discuss my daughter's progress. But she does tell me that once her daughter said she wanted to marry Daddy.

Once. Let me tell you what's been going on in my house. "Kissy, kissy, kissy," says the daughter to her father when he comes in from work. (I hasten to say she got this from Carol Burnett's Miss Hannigan in the movie "Annie," and not from her mother.) When I attempt to kiss her, she pulls away. Even when I'm successful, she wipes the kiss off. "You give wet kisses, Mommy! Yuk!" I try. I dry my mouth before I purse up. Still she pulls away. "Give me a hug," I say. She gives me a quick, grudging strangle. Daddy is embraced and kissed and massaged.

"I can hug you better, Daddy," she says. "I don't want you two to hug each other."

In the middle of the night, she's up for water. She peeks into our room. "What are you two doing in there?" in the same tone I employ when I come into her room to find her jumping on the bed with her friend. We aren't doing anything, in fact, but she senses the possibilities.

I am consoled by my friends. A mother of a five-year-old heard her daughter say, with great disdain, to a playmate, "There's a roach on the floor over there, and *she* doesn't even see it."

Another tells of lying in bed with her husband and child and receiving this imperative: "Get up and cook breakfast for me and Daddy."

She wants to kill mamma and marry daddy, say the books; don't take it seriously. Don't let her come between her parents. Don't let her think she's really a threat. And don't ever, ever let her think it's possible. It would terrify her. Me, too.

★   ★   ★

My husband is never nude these days. Towels and boxer shorts when he's dressing. Still, you can't blame him for accepting the kisses. There was a time, not long ago, when I was her great love, when she would cry if my husband picked her up at the sitter's instead of me.

Only one friend comes up with something truly consoling. Her husband weighs 300 pounds and appears as a mere toad in her son's family portrait at a school across town. Mother and son fared well in the rendering. If a 300-pound man can come to toad, the experts may know whereof they speak. And who am I, a slight 130 pounds, to complain? (On vacation, this same son suggested one motel room for his father, another for himself and his mother.)

The books say it will get better. They say it will go into latency. In another year or so I will have my daughter back until her teen years. I don't like what this word latency implies. That we all really do live in the House of Thebes, just pretending to be loving, not recognizing what is elemental, terrifying and real. And what about those teen years? I'm not sure I'm up to them. Not if her hair is as golden as it is now. Not if her eyes are still as blue and clear.

How We Sprung
For a New Mattress
(1984)

In a marriage of long standing, there is the seven-year itch
and the fifteen-year slump. The slump belongs to our mattress,
our first piece of furniture and our only one for some time.
We've taken it with us and it has taken us with it: the depres-
sions of our bodies are right there on the fern motif satin, a
large one on the left, a smaller one on the right. If I can't see
them exactly in the day, I can certainly fit into the one that
is me.

Of late, however, sprongs have jutted into all my familiar
recesses. I roll over, I twitch, I wake my husband. He takes
his pillow and goes out to the couch.

"The mattress is the message," he declares cryptically in the
morning.

I think about this during the day. The mattress is the
message... What is my husband trying to tell me? I finally relax
and decide he simply means we should get a new mattress.

Yes, this is it exactly, says my husband that evening. We
need a new mattress. A good idea. King size, this time. And
while we're at it, let's get one like that British mattress company gave Princess Di and Charles. You know, real big and
with separate springs and all, so the prince doesn't disturb her
when he comes in late from, you know, one of his parties.

Go to hell, I say.

Just kidding, he says.

Hah.

I consider his suggestion of king-size. We have a queen-size now. Even that is bigger than my parents had. A double bed was good enough for people of my parents' generation.

A cot in a dormitory was once plenty good for us.

A sleeping bag on an island in Lake George was one of the best beds we ever made.

"I would never get a king-size," says my friend who is newly wed. "I wouldn't want to be that far away from my honey." She said this with some humor, and that's why it's O.K. for me to still be her friend. I decide to go with the king-size.

That week when I strip the bed, I cast a cold eye on the mattress. It is stained with all the elixirs of our life together: menstrual blood, sweat, semen, baby pee, breast milk.

How will we get it out of the place without the neighbors seeing it? We live in an apartment building.

It's not like we can drag it out at night to a field, or leave it by the side of a stream like good countryfolk do — an anonymous mattress for kids to jump on or extremely illicit and undiscriminating lovers to lie upon. Maybe I can leave it out by the incinerator wearing its Dior morning-glory fitted sheet, which is only five years old. Since it's fitted to the queen, it will be useless when we get the king anyway.

"We'll put it out as is," says my husband, who believes he has nothing to hide. "You really think other people's mattresses don't look like this? You think we're different?"

It's my husband's idea, the new mattress, but it is I who go to a mattress store on my lunch hour. This is because I have taken the idea for my own. Nothing will do for me now but a new king-sized mattress. My husband will be glad to continue discussing the idea, but it is left to me to act if I want more than the Idea of Mattress. You learn a few things in fifteen years.

I lie on all the beds wearing my coat and boots. Some are too soft. Some are too hard. One is just right and I buy it. I am greatly relieved when the salesman assures me that I have only to give him ten more dollars and the delivery men will dispose of the old mattress for me. Small price, I think. Doesn't the store know that people would pay any price for the shame-free removal of their old mattress? I do not ask where they will take it. I choose not to know. I sign the charge slip and put the carbons in my purse.

The salesman gives me something else. It is a guarantee. A guarantee for a mattress. Can you imagine taking a mattress back? But then I remember that someone, a friend of an acquaintance (not a close friend of mine, I hasten to report), did just that. Dragged the thing back with some complaint after three years of sleep and got her money back.

I glance at the guarantee before tucking it next to the carbons. And then I look again. The mattress I have purchased is guaranteed for fifteen years! All their good mattresses are guaranteed for fifteen years, the salesman says. I conceal my amazement, arrange for a Saturday delivery, thank him and leave.

That night I get my period and stain the bed. Then it hits me cold, the way things do in the middle of the night. The mattress that gets delivered on Saturday will be the last one marked by my menses, which will cease its flow before the warranty wears out.

The seven ages of man come down to four or five mattresses. That night, I go back to bed, fit into my depression, and lie awake next to my sleeping husband, thinking about the guarantee, wondering what else will leave me or come to me during the years I lie on my new mattress.

Returning the Cat
(1983)

"Oh, Mommy, how I will love a cat!" my daughter tells me over soggy Honey Nut Cheerios. It's part of her campaign.

"Which do you wanna play," she asks that evening, coming into the kitchen with an armload of stuffed animals, "pet store, zoo, or veterinarian?" Some choice. I stir the pot of sauce and reach for my Scotch on the counter. "Pet store," I say.

She drops the animals on the floor, races to her room for her cash register, and sets up business in front of the refrigerator. "Well. Today we have some very nice little giraffes. They're very small and they have rainbows."

"Thank you for showing me these, madam. I have a small daughter and she'll like them. Give me five," I say. "How much?"

She shrugs. "Oh...eight cents only. Your small daughter will like them. And your new baby, too."

I don't have a new baby. The new baby is a sub-theme of my daughter's, after cats. My thought is this: a cat could take the pressure off and I could avoid nine months of pregnancy. My daughter would be happy. I convince my husband.

Kittens are hard to come by in the winter. I call Bide-A-Wee and the Humane Society for two weeks. Finally Bide-A-Wee has some. Eight weeks old. "Kittens downstairs," I'm told when I arrive.

I go down and check them out. No rainbows, but one is slate gray and delicate, the fur pulled taut over high aristocratic cheekbones. When it mews, I see the pink of its throat and the fretting on the roof of its mouth.

55

I'm upstairs in a minute. "The gray one."

The clerk is disapproving. "Don't you want to spend more time?"

"No." I say. I know what I know.

"How long do they last?" I ask him as I sign the adoption papers.

"Twenty-two years."

This news gives me pause. Twenty-two years is longer than most people's daughters stay at home these days. Will she take the cat when she goes? I have a flash of me and my husband watching television in our empty nest, the cat nestled at our feet. But it's too late. My name is on the line and the cat in his box. I stop at Gristede's for Nine Lives Kitty Stew on the way home. A woman on line congratulates me.

★ ★ ★

We made that cat too special. I know. I've made people too special before, too. I set my daughter up for a big surprise coming home from nursery school that day. I had the camera ready. ("You sure picked a cute one, Mom," she said, laughing delightedly before she cried as the kitten sunk its baby claws into her baby flesh for the first time.) We told everyone, as if no one in the world had ever had a cat before. We invited her friends over for viewings. We took it to school for a quick visit. We bought her cat stickers. It's where we went wrong.

The cat didn't do anything wrong. It was just a cat. From the first moment it knew to use the kitty litter. For a while it slept like a baby because it was a baby. Its mistress carried it around the place curled in an old ski hat, and both were content.

But then the cat got too big for its hat. It stopped sleeping and launched into its second life: ubiquity. High frenzied ubiquity in the evening hours when the child was bedded and we were relaxed with the paper. There is an hour in our day that is ours and, determined to have it, we retreated to the bedroom and closed the door.

The cat would follow, slapping itself upside the door and stretching its paw under, only this beseeching leg and paw visible on the bedroom rug, accompanied by a dolorous plaint and whine from the rest of the cat outside.

My husband and I have a low threshold for this sort of behavior. We started swapping sadistic cat stories. A grandfather who drowned them, a father who took them for good long walks, a friend whose nine iron made contact with the cat instead of the golf ball. One night, as the cat stories got sicker and the caterwauling more awful, we looked at the cat leg on the rug and realized: we are not cat people.

The cat soon took to biting. Still, the scratching was the real problem. It had this trick of digging into Levis and climbing up one's leg to get to lap. Better to wear jeans though. It could also work the trick on bare leg.

The child and I took a cat stool (in a Baggie) and the cat to Bide-A-Wee for a routine test. It was snowing. This is how I will spend my life, I remember thinking, premenstrually, as the bus skidded into our stop.

The vet weighed herself, then weighed herself with the cat, then subtracted her weight from the total to arrive at the cat's new weight. "He's growing nicely," she said.

And don't I know it, I thought, looking resentfully at this young tom that so recently was the kitten. My daughter, though, held him carefully as the vet gave him a shot, then, knowing from shots herself, offered comfort. "You were a good boy, yeah."

I decided to broach the subject. "What about declawing?" I asked thinly, and for support I rolled up my daughter's sleeve to expose the pitiful scabs that were her arms.

The vet was silent for a long moment. "We don't do that here." She smiled. "It's really an amputation. It takes part of their toes, too. It's not very nice. Why don't you try clipping its toenails?"

Like we hadn't. Like my husband wasn't delighted at his new duty. Like we didn't have enough toenails to clip already. "Good," said my husband that evening, as he clipped and took his scratches. "Let him keep his claws. I want him to have them to defend himself when we throw him out on Avenue C." And then he sneezed.

Because here is the other thing. My husband had been sneezing a lot. And wheezing. We're not quick, so it took us awhile to put it together. As many weeks as we had the cat, we realized finally. Now we see *a way out*. But he didn't get it checked out for a few more weeks, just sneezed and wheezed and sighed mightily when the cat came into view.

My daughter, even, was beginning to show impatience with the cat, as though it were a sibling, a naughty one, knocking over blocks, pouncing on dolls. "Let's put it in the bathroom," she'd say. The cat was spending more and more time in exile.

And then news from the allergist: positive. We sat down and talked to our daughter. She's a smart kid. Talk it out, we figured, and then she'll be okay.

"Daddy's allergic."

"The cat makes me sick, honey."

"We love the cat, but we love Daddy more than the cat, don't we?"

"Are you sure it's Daddy?" she asked after we finished.

"What?"

She began to cry. "Are you sure it's Daddy and not a man wearing a mask?" she asked, and the question chilled me.

I dropped her off at school and returned home to the cat, who greeted me guilelessly, sidling up against my ankle like things were fine. Do the deed, I told myself. I got the card-board cat carrier provided by Bide-A-Wee. "Bring home a little love," it says on the outside. The cat knew. It protested as I folded down the flaps.

And then, as a parting shot, it stuck a claw out and scratched my leather jacket. I paid too much money for my leather jacket. It is soft Italian leather, aviator style. I wear it everywhere, with everything. It reminds me, especially on days such as this, that I am hip. And now it will always remind me of the cat.

"Do you have an appointment to bring back this cat?" the clerk asked.

"No, I don't, but my husband is allergic and..."

"Do you wish to abandon this cat?" I took this question to be a little snotty, especially since, on the wall behind the clerk, is a sign that says "There is a fine of $500 for abandoning animals in New York City."

"No," I said, but held my ground and played dumb. "I don't know what to do. I have no choice. My husband is allergic. I can't bring it back home." The clerk either took pity or figured that this stupid woman was going to be hanging around his desk all day. He wrote me up a cat release form. Following procedure, I took it up to the vet. The vet was sympathetic and sorry for my little girl. She assured me that the cat would not be destroyed, that it was young enough to be adopted quickly and adapt well.

I was a free woman, I thought. But my daughter cried in nursery school. We bought a rodent that very afternoon, and she likes it. But she still has questions.

"Who will have my cat?" ("The vet will take it home with her," I said. "She loves cats and there will be other cats for it to play with.")

"Will she know to give it the same name? Otherwise it might get confused."

"Do you think it misses me?"

"Do you miss my cat?"

"Why can't Daddy take medicine?"

"Will it love the vet more than it loves me? Can we go visit the vet?"

It has been a year. Though she doesn't ask the questions as often, she still asks. Last week, for instance, she asked one. "Guess who my favorite cat is?"

Halloween in New York
(1988)

You are a child in New York. It is early October. You and
your parents are walking off a 6th Street tandoori dinner,
headed north on First. At the restaurant, you dined next to
a young man in a peplumed cossack uniform, whose hair had
been done in a thick French braid. His date was a milkmaid
in her Ukrainian peasant blouse and dirndl. A woman in a
sari bade you good bye as a man in an awesome white turban
and jamah held the door for you.

Out on the street again, you are nearly taken home by a
biker wearing a cape, who apparently cannot see beyond the
brim of his silver-starred sombrero. A man in a white robe,
his head covered with a hand-crocheted topi, leaves the mosque
on 11th, and Santa Claus passes on his way to Veniero's
bakery. Santa, still in his warm-weather look (a red T-shirt
and ponytail), greets you and tells you to select a pair of earrings
from his card of dime-store gems. A Rastafarian and skinheads
go by in turn. You pass a beckoning storefront fortune-teller,
and then the dragon lady with Fu Manchu nails, who today
has sequin-studded fuschia flames blazing from each eye.

Your walk home makes you think of something. "Mom,"
you say, as you wait for the light at 14th. "Could you buy me
a pink wig? I'm gonna go as a punk for Halloween."

Your mom doesn't say "Sure." She just laughs. Your dad
laughs, too. Your mom says, "I think there's something funny about what you just said." You are only nine, but you get
it, and you laugh out loud with your parents, even though

61

you know the joke's on you. On you and every other New
York kid at Halloween.

It's not fair!

It isn't just that everybody is always dressed up in New York
anyway. There are other things. Submerged in your unconscious is this memory of the time your parents took you
to the Village Halloween parade when you were only three.
You sat on the curb on Bleecker Street (it was a thing still
possible in those days, when you and the parade were new),
and you chatted up witches and Draculae — the ones in the
parade and the ones sitting there on the curb with you. Then
your parents pushed you through the streets of the Village,
behind the woman whose mask and shoes and coat were on
backward so it looked as though she were going to walk over
you and your stroller, but she kept walking ahead. Just like
you and your mother and father...ahead to the spooky
Jefferson Market library, where a giant tarantula crawled up
the tower and people were ladling up dark drinks from pump-
kin punch bowls by the light of black candelabra. Even though
you were very small then and everything seemed big, Halloween seemed very, very big.

Your mom tells you about Halloween in her small hometown:
how the kids would go out by themselves at night, blocks and
blocks away from home, just running wild in a pack, up to
each porch with its jack-o'-lantern, and then home way after
dark with bags full of treats. She says she got to eat everything,
too, especially the delicious homemade stuff: brownies, candy
apples, popcorn balls, marshmallow Rice Krispie squares — the
exact same stuff that she *throws out* now because it isn't
hermetically sealed and therefore contains razor blades.

Also, she got to stay up as late as she wanted on Halloween
because she went to Catholic school, which was always closed
the next day for All Soul's Day. "All Soul's Day was the true

holiday for us," she says. "All Hallows' Eve, the night before, means holy night." And then she says, "Wait a minute, the true meaning is pagan!" When you ask her what's pagan, she starts to tell you, then says, "Skip it." Anyway, all she had to do the next day was go to Mass and say ejaculations to earn indulgences for the souls of the dear departed and then she could go home and lump out and eat fudge squares. You don't even bother to ask what's ejaculations.

Your mom says nobody cared too much about costumes. There wasn't this pressure to be creative. All you had to do was pull a stocking over your head, or burn a cork so you could dirty up your face with it and go as a bum. Go as a *bum*, Mom? Rad.

And she says that people always opened up their doors. They were afraid not to because kids would soap their windows. And when they did open their doors, they pretended to be afraid of the kids in their costumes. But a lot of people in New York are really afraid to open their doors. They don't even look through their peepholes. But you know they're in there because you hear Tom Brokaw talking, and so you say, "Trick or treat" very politely and hopefully. They still don't open. (Once you caught a lady getting off the elevator. "Trick or Treat," you said. She said, "Wait here." Then locked her door and never came back.) You can't soap windows because apartment doors have none, and it certainly doesn't seem very scary when you've seen other stuff you could mention.

But the worst part about Halloween in New York is having to drag the parents along with you. You wouldn't mind so much if they just escorted you, but no. Parents in New York act like kids, competing with their children, always wanting to steal the show. It's why they came to New York in the first place. If they wanted to be grown-ups, they would have stayed in their hometowns when they got big. But instead they came to never-never land. Your mom says they called it Fun City in those days, so that's why she's here. Halloween is their chance to act out. Your mom was a leopard last year. Her Clown White makeup has lasted her for years. Another mother in the playground tells your mom that she's going to rent a Marie Antoinette costume from a costume company. Also, they always have to stop in and have a drink somewhere instead of trying to hit as many apartments as possible.

And there was the year that your friend Stuart (not his real name) from six (not his real floor) joined you with his dad, James (not his name either). You were glad to see Stuart, but James is six feet tall and he was wearing (what else?) a stocking over his head with this gash and stitches painted on it. Actually, it was panty hose, but he had one leg draped around his neck, also a noose. He was drinking a Budweiser. He said "Trick or treat" in this slow, low voice. Hardly anyone opened the door that year because James was the only thing they could see through the peep-hole. Your mom tried to reason with him. She said, "Damn it, James, could you at least hide until they open the door? Could you do that, huh, James, let women and children go first? Or how 'bout you give us Stuart and you can go trick-or-treating after we're done?" But would he? No. He laughed and said what people could do about it if they were scared. He liked it that he was scaring people, and he didn't think of us kids at all.

It's enough to make you want to pull a stocking over your head.

Confessions of
a Corporate Wife
(1989)

I once was a frequent flyer for free, if anything can be said
to be free. I was an itinerant corporate wife. Should I use the
politically correct term "corporate spouse," or its plural, spice?
But spice would not be precise. Sadly, it was the rare male on
these trips who was a corporate husband, who attended such
spouse sessions as "Morning Exercise Workout with Body by
Jake" or "Diane Sawyer, Who Will Address her Journalism
Career."

I am still a wife, though no longer on the road. The times,
the job, my husband, and I have changed. During the few years
of my tenure, though, I went to Maui, Westchester, Tucson,
Southern California (three times), Cape Cod, Bermuda, the
Catskills, Paris, the Riviera, West Virginia, Key West, the
Helmsley, and St. Thomas. These were reward trips, or incen-
tive trips. I went, even though I believe there are people in
occupations far more deserving of rewards or incentives than
those of corporate executives: coal miners, domestic workers,
hospital orderlies. But the trips were offered to me and I went.
I confess, I was seduced, at least at first. You would be too,
if it happened to you. At least at first.

For the first trip I was all new. I smiled continually, attended
every function, and wore my name tag all four days. All my
cocktail dresses were new, bought in a frenzy the week before
at the late Emotional Outlet. I even had an actual outfit to
wear on the plane. By the third trip, however, I took to stuffing

the same old things in the bag. And then, finally, *I turned down a trip to Hawaii* because it conflicted with a "Let's All Sing Together" concert my daughter and I were in at The Third Street Music School. A friend said, "What a good mother!" but the truth was, I preferred singing "Consider Yourself At Home."

Lest you think me entirely jaded, there are certainly moments I look back on. Well I remember, approaching the Riviera, how the tour bus listed dangerously to the right as husbands rushed from their wives' sides to check out the topless beaches. My husband maintained his dignity and my respect. He was already seated on the right. ("Topless! Before noon!" a woman remarked.)

Also, I have to say, Tucson's Beach Boys concert in a dark desert, a cactus-covered cliff as a backdrop, with 700 grown-ups wearing fluorescent necklaces, dancing in thunder and lightning to "Little Old Lady from Pasadena" *was* pretty darn memorable.

I remember the wonderful afternoon in Paris when we lunched at a café and visited the Orangerie while our entourage went for the scheduled hot air balloon rides over the French countryside. Our reasons for skipping that event are as follows:

We wanted to see the "Water Lilies" again.

We didn't think we'd like to balloon with name tags.

We'd rather not balloon with a hundred people.

It seemed too much of an American invasion, and we had already done that to the French countryside.

We were recovering from the French theme party of the night before, where men were given black berets, women red ones, as favors. The band had played "New York, New York" and "I Love Paris" relentlessly, and the evening ended with the assembled, standing and bereted, singing "God Bless America" to a Statue of Liberty carved from butter.

I have my regrets. I have never in this life, before or since, been offered an opportunity to hot air balloon over anywhere. And I was told it was just a ball! But I couldn't.

In Maui we were all issued camouflage T-shirts to wear to the M.A.S.H. theme beach party: jeeps, tents, a helicopter, announcements, the chaplain walking around blessing everyone. I wore a lei and something pink (feminine, I suppose) and stood out against hundreds of people in camouflage. That's not why I did it. I just didn't really think *everyone* would wear those T-shirts when they had brought nice clothes. When people asked me, I said I was dressing in drag, like Corporal Klinger.

I remember meeting Earl (not his name). It was at "A Night at the Circus" under the big top somewhere in West Virginia. We had been greeted by a calliope, given popcorn by clowns and cotton candy by the ringmaster. People took pictures of each other inside a lion's cage. Before the circus parade began, we repaired to our ringside tables and dinner. As Earl pulled out the balloon-festooned chair next to mine, he smiled and greeted our table with a hearty: "The wife's not here tonight, so I guess I can tell wife jokes." I pointed out that I was a wife. That didn't stop Earl. I guess his wife was the only one that counted. Each time he began a joke, I would say, "I heard that one." But that didn't stop Earl either. Also he had things to say about the woman on the flying trapeze. Here's one of Earl's jokes: "A woman needs four animals: a mink for her back, a jaguar for her garage, a tiger in bed, and a jackass to pay for it all." Speaking of animals, the favors for "A Night at the Circus" included a variety of plastic animal noses that are held in place with a rubber band: pig snouts, elephant trunks, beaks. Guess which kind Earl got?

I liked most of the people on these trips a lot better than I liked Earl. I remember some of them, and some of them fondly, though I can't say whether I met them in Florida or Bermuda.

That's what happens. One's memory of these trips gets generic. All the places become the same place, all the hotels the same. The polite cocktail conversations, the orgiastic Farewell Champagne Buffet Brunches have melted with the chocolates left on the bed by the turn-down service. Where was that Pirate Theme Party anyway? St. Thomas or Key West? And where was it that we fled from Rich Little's after-dinner monologue? Where were the fireworks? And what about that wild and crazy night with the Pointer Sisters?

I can, however, recall quite easily the times that we went AWOL, to see Joshua trees and coyotes in Southern California, or kamikaze surfers on a wild beach in Maui; the drive we took to a volcanic crater at dawn or the visit with a poet friend in Tucson.

But there are other trips with far more staying power. I can telescope to them over fifteen or twenty years. Flashes of them console me on the subway or in the dentist's chair. The taste of well-done burgers cooked over a Coleman stove in the presence of a moose on an Oregon beach. The blizzard in Montana one July. The ceramic cherubs on the mantle, guarding our $7.00-per-night room in a pensione on Rue Des Ecole. The afternoon tea in County Sligo, when a shocked fellow traveler said: "I *never* thought I'd see an American woman take a second scone!"

These journeys had this in common. We went by ourselves and we paid our own money, though usually not much.

Reading to the Literate
(1989)

We are a reading family. Recently a child stayed with us for the weekend and afterward reported us to her parents: "All they did was read." The big motherhood breakthrough came for me when my daughter was six and we took a train journey together. I was resigned to the prospect of entertaining her for the duration with stories and walks to the Club Car for chips. Instead, she read to herself, a book with actual chapters in it, *Ramona Quimby*. We sat together reading for three hours. I recognized the significance of the moment even as I lived it: I was as I had once been, a woman free to read her own stuff.

And yet, though she's nine now and an excellent reader, we persist in reading aloud to her a few times a week. Is it a sick attempt to fix her at six? Are we clinging unhealthily to a vestige of her early childhood? Is reading aloud to an easy reader a pathological act?

But, consider, if you don't read to a child when she's big, she might not have a memory of having been read to, and memory is all. Oh, sure, sure, she might have a psychic memory of it, but how useful is that? It's not a conscious memory. You as a parent will not get credit for it later. There's no way she's going to remember being read *Pat the Bunny!* How could she? She was *too little!* As an adult, she won't be able to tell her friends, "My parents screwed up a lot, but, gee, I remember they always read me *Pat the Bunny*." No. You have to get kids when they're older if you want the experience to have staying power. The memory of having been read to is a solace one carries through adulthood. It can wash over a multitude of parental sins. I have seen it again and again. Even people with really rotten parents wax elegiac when they recall being read to, the funny voices their parents adopted, the book that was so special, the physical closeness that they felt.

Body contact is an important reason for reading to the older child. Cuddling with Mom or Dad gets phased out in pre-adolescence, and reading together is a perfect excuse to have that sweet warm body in quietude near yours for half an hour.

Also it beats playing board games. When she suggests Ruffhouse or Checkers, I say, "What about *Little Women?*" There's dignity in reading and none whatever in having repeatedly to king your own issue. You get respect as a reader that you never get playing checkers with a child. You can, for instance, demonstrate that you know a lot of big words. You can point out how wise Marmee is, and how well her daughters obey her. If you've read the book already, you know what's going to happen, which gives you an important edge. I know, for instance, when Beth is going to die, and who Laurie is going to marry. Having lived through Beth's death some thirty years ago, maybe I'll be able to get through it this time and be a rock for my daughter.

Maybe. But my fear is that I'm really going to lose it when Beth dies, even more than I have already in our sessions. Be warned. A lachrymal tendency is loosed in a parent when reading to a child. It is as D.H. Lawrence wrote, ". . . cast down in the flood of remembrance, I weep like a child for the past." For a past when these books were my books, when someone read them to me, or more likely, didn't read them to me.

Another wellspring for tears is the sharing of life's sorrows. You never want this child to know sadness, and yet here it is, on the page, before you both. She has rarely seen me cry about real life, yet when I read, she recognizes the early emotion in my rising voice before my actual tears: "Are you about to cry, Mom?" I always am.

I've mourned the death of a spider:

". . . none of the new spiders ever quite took her place in his heart. She was in a class by herself. It is not often that someone comes along who is a true friend and a good writer. Charlotte was both." (*Charlotte's Web*, E. B. White)

And a poignant father-son swan scene:

"Louis wanted to thank his father but he was unable to say a word. And he knew it would do no good to write 'Thank you' because his father wouldn't be able to read it, never having had an education. So Louis just bobbed his head and waggled his tail and fluttered his wings. The cob knew by these signs that he had found favor in the sight of his son. . ." (*The Trumpet of the Swan*, E. B. White)

I began weeping before *Anne of Green Gables* even began, during the foreword, which recounted the hard, orphaned life of Lucy Maud Montgomery, Anne's creator: "My inner life has been lived entirely alone. Sometimes I am conscious of a great soul loneliness."

Sometimes *Anne of GG* lagged for me, especially the way the plot hinged on whether Anne would pass the entrance exam for Queen's, or win the Avery scholarship. Was there ever a doubt? My daughter, however, wrote of Anne in a school book report: "I liked her because she touched my heart." And that touched my heart. I like to think that it was more than the book. It was the sum of our hearts.

I hope I've established that reading to the already literate is not pathological. But you wouldn't call it altruistic either.

My One and Only, and Why
(1989)

I have an only child. She is two digits now, and beautiful, talented, smart and very funny. These are facts, though I who am her mother relate them. You will have to take it on faith. She loves animals, other children, *The Babysitters Club*, and Debbie Gibson. She hates fur coats and parties filled with rowdy adults. She holds doors open for old people. She is greatly concerned about the Brazilian rain forests and the Valdez oil spill.

When she was two, some people started making sounds about my having another. I dealt with them summarily: I cut my eyes at them, giving them a glance that was on the dark side of withering, though I stopped short of sticking out my tongue. This is no better treatment than a nosybody deserves in any case, but my case wasn't any case.

We all have our own stories, and this is mine. I grew up in the largest family I knew, the eldest of ten chidren. After that experience, there is *no way* I would ever have a second child! I feel greatly privileged to have this one. She is more than I ever wished for myself in my fondest dream of hope. So why would I ever want another?

In fact, I almost didn't have her, and my heart stops cold when I think of it.

My husband and I were married years before I ever got pregnant. Fun years, yes. (And I was so determined to have fun in those years!) But in the middle of all this fun, we would sometimes stop and ask the question: Should we? Or not? My husband always let me answer it. In my early twenties I took a hard line: "Kids? Arghh! Who wants 'em? I've had it to here with kids! Let's go to Paris and drink Cote du Rhône." And we did. As I got older, though, I would agonize over it, lie awake at night obsessing about it. Yes or no? Yes or no? Yes or no? And then I would say no. There was never, actually, a moment when I said yes. I like to think that my unconscious, knowing what was good for me, drank Cote du Rhône one night and let it all happen. We celebrated our eleventh wedding anniversary on the maternity ward.

How could I be other than ambivalent? It's a built-in conflict. I was raised to be a nurturer, but I was tired of nurturing. Actually, I believe that ambivalence is the sign of intelligent life. It is what separates us from guinea pigs and cows, who seem quite sure of their direction. And why wouldn't anyone be ambivalent about a decision that promises immeasurable yet intangible, vague rewards, but requires physical and emotional pain, the expenditure of tens of thousands of dollars, years of restricted mobility, and untold hours of hard work? Most of my friends have had at least some ambivalence about having children. That is, once they got past their ambivalence about getting married.

But I believe that I was one of the most baby-ambivalent women ever actually to give birth. There are psychologists who say that morning sickness is a sign of ambivalence. They say the woman is actually trying to throw up the baby! Now I will allow that there is such a thing as a psychosomatic illness, but, boy, was I angry the first time I heard that one! "Just one more theory that lays the blame on the woman," I ranted to anyone who would listen. "Imagine! Here you are, sick as a dog, and they're telling you you're trying to throw up the baby!" But...was I being defensive? Because the truth is I had one of the longest-running cases of morning sickness on record: seven months, far beyond the first trimester, when most morning sickness disappears.

I, who had changed hundreds of diapers by the time I was sixteen, found having a child the hardest thing I ever did.

Is it unfair? Does she need a sibling? Is there too much pressure on her? Am I depriving her because of my own schtick? This may be, but she seems to be thriving. There's a lot to be said for only child-dom. Check out the astronauts and any Harvard Business School class. (I hasten to add that these are not my goals for her.) She has expressed the wish for a sibling, but less and less of late. Her first cousins are very important to her. And she has many friends to whom she is fiercely devoted. As I say, we each have our own story. This is hers. And if these things go in cycles, she may end up the mother of a brood, and I the grandmother. I could be a wonderful grandmother to many children. I would remember their birthdays and play bouncy-bouncy when I came to visit. And then I would go home.

There are delights to a large family, to be sure. When I was growing up, I thought our family was special. Certainly everyone told me it was wonderful, and how lucky I was. (It was very smart of me, I realize now, to think it was wonderful at the time I was a part of it.) You didn't need dolls because there was always a real baby. You learned not to be squeamish. You learned an awareness (though not always a sympathy) for the other guy. You always had company. If you decided to direct "Cinderella," you could always bully your siblings into being the mice. As an adult, you will never really be alone in the world (though you may sometimes feel alone). I am trying to think of other delights, but I cannot.

Of course, when there were joys, there were many people to share them, and that is true of the sorrows also. But I have come to believe that any very large family has more sorrows, unique sorrows; they are deep ones, they are many, and they hurt. Even if there is enough money, as there was in my family, there is still no escaping a spiritual neediness. Not even the best, most giving parents have enough attention to give to each of these children.

A large family affects your self-image. With all these people who look just the same as you, it's hard not to feel somewhat expendable. You think: why am I not good enough for my parents? Why did there have to be so many? Sibling rivalry is heightened exponentially by all those siblings. Children often get labels which they are expected to live by: Mommy's Little Helper; Witchie; Bump on a Log; Mike Tyson; El Studioso; Fat, But a Pretty Face; The Dumb Ox. (Only kidding, but you get the idea.) If one sibling succeeds, and another does not, there is a kind of survivor guilt. There is very little privacy, and, in fact, privacy is highly suspect. Keeping a diary is a kamikaze act. There are endless grueling maintenance tasks. (Just consider one thing, say, the Herculean effort it takes each November to make sure each child has boots that fit.) And there is always the worry, the continual worry about all the others that you carry with you wherever you go.

I do not have enough maternal, hard-core love in me for more than one child. I spent my childhood loving lots of children as my own, and it left me a little drained in the love department. It left me a little needy. If I still needed so much love and attention myself, how could I ever give it? In fact, I was stingy with it in my daughter's earliest years. Though I did love her, I resented what seemed to be constant demands. I wanted other people to help me with her. I stayed awake at night. I went into therapy. I took tranquilizers. "I have to get away," I would say, and often did. I went back to work when she was very young. I sometimes let her cry too long without picking her up. When she was only a few months old, my mother-in-law flew up from Florida to take her for a week so that I could "relax."

And then something happened. She taught me, this daughter. (And no mistake, the therapy helped plenty.) As she grew, she grew on me. I had always been told what love is, who you must love, the duty it implies. But I love this girl freely. I love her madly. When I see how much she's grown, I fervently wish I could have her early years back to lavish her with the attention I couldn't give her then. I have forgiven myself these early years. I was who I was, and I couldn't be otherwise, because I had come from a particular place. And the first years of any baby's life are stressful for a new mother. But I know now what I didn't know then. She is not another sibling crowding me out, but my own sweet child, the only one I will ever have.

Slouching Toward Vegetarianism
(1989)

Roast beast, my brother Kevin called it, and we ate it nearly every Sunday growing up. My mother faithfully took its temperature, so the standing rib roast was always perfect: rare and bloody in the center, brown and crisp on the outside, salty drippings and fat in the pan, something for everyone in the large Irish-American family I came from. Like her mother before her, my mother would boast how she made the butcher give her the first cut. If we had guests, my mother would accept compliments on behalf of the cow: "That's a lovely piece of meat, Ann!" or "What a gorgeous roast!" The beast was always accompanied by potatoes browned in its fat. Meat and potatoes, that's what we were, and no bones about it.

Like my mother before me, I brought this heritage to my bridal china, after picking me out a meat-and-potatoes kind of guy. Our weekly menu read like this: baconburgers, hot dogs, stew, hamburgers, veal cutlets, hot dogs, cheeseburgers. And for company, of course, roast beef, though I would serve Yorkshire pudding in place of potatoes. We managed to come through the seventies and Woodstock untainted by any intimations of vegetarianism. We had the "War is not healthy for children and other living things" poster, but we thought it meant butterflies and bluebirds and flowers, not pigs. My husband once even went so far as to order a stew de petit lapin for Easter brunch!

But this marriage has produced a daughter more moral and large-of-heart than either of its parts; a daughter who, at the age of nine, is firm in her resolve. She knows what she wants and what she loves. She loves animals and won't eat them. She has caused a revolution in our household. "It's only a phrase," my mother-in-law said. I took comfort and thought of my brother Gerard, who at twelve announced that he would never eat another land animal. He defined land animals as those who walked on four legs. Chicken was edible. Still, I worried about Gerard. How would he live? I lectured him on the need for protein. I bought him vitamins. Then my mother made meatballs. Gerard stared at the dwindling pile of meat-balls (they go fast in a large family) and finally took a stab at one. "That's one good son-of-a-gun land animal!" he said, to our great relief.

But Nora has not eaten meat for more than a year. At first I was as freaked out by this as I had been by Gerard and his land-animal stance. But she seems to be living, even thriving. It is a great sacrifice, because when she was younger, she loved meat, especially steak. But this Thanksgiving she gave up the turkey, and wouldn't even eat the stuffing that had been in it or the gravy that she used to love. If she's at a birthday party and they're serving hot dogs, she goes without. Since, like many children, she doesn't care for many vegetables and exotic fare, her diet is extremely limited. "It's boring!" she complains, sometimes, but she eats it, again and again and again. Peanut butter on whole wheat, pizza, and macaroni and cheese.

Vegetarianism is damn inconvenient, I say as cook. It means you can't go to Burger King anymore, or throw a steak on the grill. It means labor-intensive cooking if you want something good, and I do want Nora to have some meals she really enjoys. It means deconstructing cookbooks to learn a whole new vocabulary of foods: tritiflour, complementary proteins, tempeh, lentils, soy, brown rice. It means trying to disguise the taste of tofu. It means that I've had precious few successes with the recipes I've attempted in recent months. My gado gado sauce was a disaster disaster, attributable, I believe, to my confusion of coconut creme with coconut milk. (I dared to undertake the recipe in the first place because I had a familiarity with coconut creme from all the pina coladas I've slung into the blender.)

After all this trouble, I'm damned if I'll make a second meal for the carnivores in residence. When we do have meat, we feel guilty eating it in front of Nora. So we often don't. We eat our meat in restaurants these days, but not without guilt. Even without Nora there, we cannot escape the new awareness she brought to us: *we are eating flesh, dead animal.* Sure it's good, it's delicious, but there's the guilt.

There are payoffs to our new lifestyle, however. We all lost weight, several pounds. (In part because food just isn't that important anymore.) Our food bill is much smaller. We feel fine, and there are experts who tell us we'll live longer.

I told my friend, call her Sally, an animal rights activist, our story. She was delighted that the righteousness of a child should be visited upon her parents. When I saw her for lunch, she ordered split pea soup and gave me a letter to Nora, telling her how proud she was of her, and that she's bragging about this wonderful child to all her animal rights friends. The letter contained a pin of Bossy with the big brown eyes and the imperative, "MORE THAN MEAT! GO VEGETARIAN!" which Nora wears on her denim jacket next to the pin that says "HOMEWORK CAUSES BRAIN DAMAGE."

Sally also requested that an animal rights group send Nora a newsletter. We inspected it before showing it to Nora. Among the items was the observation that eggs cry when they're taken from the hen. The newsletter got censored down the garbage chute. I have since heard a report that eggs cry when you open the refrigerator, saying, I suppose, in some egsoteric language, *Not me, not me! Take him, take him!* I have listened for the eggs in my fridge. I have held a condemned egg up to my ear. I did not hear its cry. There are those, I know, who would say I did not hear its cry because I am not listening properly, because I do not want to. They would say I have turned a deaf ear to the cries of eggs, and I am not sure I can deny their accusations.

This is a question I am left with. Where do you draw the line? At eggs? At land animals? At fish? At anything that reproduces? Amoebae, then. Are you allowed to cheat and make risotto with chicken broth or have a bit of pepperoni on your pizza or bacon on your spinach salad?

Sally also had a present for me that day, one she didn't want Nora to see: a fat manila envelope which contained before, during, and after pictures of slaughtered animals. "Don't look at these before you go to sleep!" she warned. I put it on my bureau waiting for a good time to look at it. Before I ate? Or after? Upon arising, whilst summoning the requisite cheer to face a new day? "When you look at these pictures, I guarantee, you'll never, ever eat meat again!" said Sally. And I know that's true. Which is why the envelope stayed on top of my bureau for two weeks, then went down the chute unopened. It's like St. Augustine, I think it was, said to God on another matter: "Lord, make me chaste, but not yet."

IF BEAUTY IS TRUTH, TELL IT

My Mane Man
The Tressful Tale of T.
(1988)

I know my head was turned by the endless possibilities of New York. Like Thomas Wolfe before me, I believed that fulfillment was waiting everywhere, and "I did not know where to go to find it, on which of the city's thousand corners it would come to me..." If I kept looking, I would find the one who would make me radiant. I was bored, I guess, searching for finesse and mastery, when really, my needs were more blunt.

It was part of the reason I left T., whom I'd been with for three years. Oh, there were other things. T. was just a neighborhood guy and I felt the tug of 57th Street. When I see T. on my block, I feel the old guilt and regret. I saw him today, as clean-cut as ever. He started to avert his eyes, but then he couldn't. I know he couldn't resist. He wanted to check me out, to see how I was looking these days without him.

I decided to speak, though sometimes we've passed each other as strangers. I can't bear that. Not after all our talks, the intimacies we've exchanged. "Hi, T.," I said. He smiled broadly at me and nodded.

That's what I remember most about T.: his generosity, so evident in his smile. I make excuses to myself all over again...his place really wasn't all that kempt, magazines all over and smelling of chemicals, no place to put your stuff, nothing comfortable to slip into. He never gave me anything to drink. But more important, he held himself too cheaply. He did not know his worth. Since he did not, how could I?

I was younger then, callow. And when he started talking permanent, I just got scared. (I'd tried it before and it didn't take.)

I went on to J. J. is dark and European, with a great accent. He was everything T. was not. J. knew the importance of preliminaries. He spent a lot of time before, looking at me in the mirror, running his fingers through my hair, massaging my scalp, asking me how I wanted it, how many inches and all. He plied me with coffee and white wine. And his place! It was really nice...pastels, different shades of pink. Sleek Formica counters with pots and pots of narcissus. He had someone clean up after. And you always got a pretty smock all washed and ironed after the last woman. I stayed with him for a year, until I began to notice how much his flash and extravagant ways were costing me. Really, I became quite sensitive then. Maybe I was looking for an excuse, but on the day I realized the bangs weren't long enough anymore, I walked.

I saw J. once after that, in a boutique on Madison, but it wasn't at all like seeing T. I got the distinct impression that J. didn't even recognize me!

I then met with disaster in the person of H. I've warned all my friends about H. I told them H. was a sadist and that they should never, *ever* let that man near them with a scissors. I told them my story as I tell you now, so that you will be warned: On my first and only encounter with H. I explained about my cowlick in the back. He told me it wasn't a cowlick, it was a swirl. I took his euphemism for kindliness, when he was actually being contrary. "I'm afraid you'll get too close," I specifically said. "I can't have that exposed." He came within a hairsbreadth, and when I protested, he acted as though it were *my* problem. "Why are you so upset?" he asked menacingly, adding that it was just a shingle, that he'd given plenty of women shingles before me!

I was a long time recovering from H. I could hardly even bring myself to use gel. For the longest time I felt no impulse or need for anyone new. And after that, I was indiscriminate, going in just about anywhere to get a quick wash and blow.

But now, seeing T. again, I wonder, as I have before, if he'd take me back.

Oh, T.! You weren't flamboyant, but you were always even; never any headtrips. You always had time for me. I didn't even need an appointment. Remember how we first met? I just stopped in the day John Lennon was murdered. It was so cold and rainy, and I was miserable. We talked about Lennon and the Beatles and how sad we both were. You didn't want to charge me because it was only bangs. But I gave you a five-dollar tip, remember? That was when you were in the old place above the drugstore. I followed you to your new place...how long ago was that?

And when I had my baby and no sitter, you jostled her carriage and sang her rock-a-bye while I had a manicure. Imagine...a new mother with a manicure! What a lift that was! And then, when the baby got a little older, you gave her her first haircut. You sat her on two phonebooks, took her picture, gave her a lollipop, and me a lock of her hair. How could I have left you because you only charged nine dollars? I know now that more isn't better. I know more isn't you, T.

T.! Let me come home again. Though I've always been so straight, I'll get kinky if you say so. And when I grow old, I'll come to you for bluing. I promise, T., Please!

The Flawed Ones
(1988)

"Your face isn't your own until you're forty," the adage from the School of Small Comfort goes. I, who have recently come into full possession of my face, am concerned for future generations. There are people in this world, people who have already been born, who may never own their own faces, who may have a hard time even knowing when they're forty!

There is a brave new world of cavity-free, wrinkle-free folk reaching maturity who give a new, true meaning to the term Beautiful People. They drank fluoridated water from birth and had protective sealants painted on their adult teeth just as soon as they got them. These Beautiful People always knew enough to stay out of the midday sun or else wear number 48 sunscreen. They were educated early and often about the ravages of drink and cigarettes and caffeine, and they accept Tofutti as a dessert.

The baby boom generation is the last of a tainted strain. How will we, the Flawed Ones, appear to our progeny when we are in our eighties? Will they be respectful and treat us as quaint antiques, or abandon us as repellent reminders of a benighted age?

My personal fight against flaw has focused on the eye area since a junior high creative writing class I taught last month. "Describe me," I told the class, thinking this would help them describe others in their writing, help them notice detail. I poised my chalk ingenuously against the board and awaited their responses to my person. The first one, from a twelve-year-old Beautiful Person (male):

"You have baggy eyes." He mistook my incredulous expression for a request for further elaboration: "Well, you know, you've got these deep lines when you smile and all, and it's kind of puffy."

I told my friend Pat, who is also in possession of her face. She said she had found an emollient for baggy eyes at the cosmetic counter, or rather two emollients, that you put on in sequence, and in sequence cost her 100 smackers. "I'd never believe it," she said, "but it works!" I've never spent more at any one cosmetic counter than I needed to in order to get the free gift, but I'm at Macy's the next Saturday morning, in a fever to be parted from my hundred. I am accompanied in this madness by my girl-child, age eight, one of the Beautiful People.

Another Beautiful Person is behind the counter. She is in her early twenties and doesn't have baggy eyes. She doesn't have baggy anything. It isn't that easy to make my purchase because she is that rare thing, a laissez-faire cosmetic saleswoman, and I can't remember the names of the unguents. She only knows about one eye product, not two. She becomes even more uninterested in my crow's feet when a youth of her acquaintance in a leather jacket and tight jeans approaches, greets her with estatic lasciviousness, and perches upon one of the pastel high chairs at the counter, from which he eagerly observes her every move. My child, oblivious to the glorious lust charging the air between these two, is in the other high chair smudging on eyeshadow. I miserably pursue my line of questioning, anxious to purchase the second product and be gone. It is too humiliating. Finally, we settle on something as the young man desultorily points out the advantages of Mauve Gold over Mid Plum to my daughter.

That same day I go home to a magazine story on aging: you don't have to age, not even us Flawed Ones. An octogenarian wrote a book called *A Dud at 70, a Stud at 80*. And there's something called Retin-A that can reverse photo-aging, excellent for crow's feet. The inventor of Retin-A scorns the eye-area preparations sold at cosmetic counters, the very stuff I've just purchased, saying they have a temporary effect, but are disastrous after years of use.

I call up Pat. "Hey," I go. "I spend all this money, and now this dermatologist says the stuff's a disaster years from now."

"*Years* from now? I only care about tomorrow morning."

★　★　★

I listen to Dr. David Orentreich on Health Saturday on WMCA, a call-in on "Retin-A for Wrinkles and Sun Damage." A lot of Flawed Ones call in. Eddie from Queens asks him about liver spots. Peggy from Long Island is seventy-six and has vertical lines at the top of her lips and at the top of her eyebrows. Lucille from Brooklyn has small whiteheads and also wants to know if she goes to the dermatologist, will she have to go with all her make-up off. (Answer, from Dr. O: You can take your make-up off when you get there.) Can Retin-A help these people? Dr. Orentreich says yes.

The Flawed Ones, ever skeptical but ever hopeful, will try Retin-A as their parents tried Geritol when Arthur Godfrey told them to. The Flawed Ones are old enough to know there are no miracles, but the sentiment among them is: what the hell, you don't have to go under the knife, do you? Also they reason that if they go into their Retin-Eighties, albeit with fillings and crowns, but with taut skin and liver-spot-free faces that aren't their own, maybe the Beautiful People won't feel the need to put them out on the ice.

The Nose Job
(1987)

I am on the phone with my friend Lisa (not her real name), whom I've not seen in a while. We've covered the time between — kids, men, jobs, the ozone layer — and now I'm telling her my retort to the man who screamed at me because I was swimming in the fast lane. "Don't make me laugh," she says, "My bandages will come out."

"Bandages?" I ask.

"I had a nose job."

My story is forgotten.

LISA GOT A NOSE JOB!

LISA WAS GORGEOUS BEFORE.

MEN WERE CRAZY ABOUT LISA EVEN WITH THE OLD NOSE.

But Lisa is still talking. Her nose had been broken in an accident in college. "My plastic surgeon told me that there were more fractures in my nose than he had ever seen on anyone who wasn't a cadaver."

"Oh," I say, and then: "I'm going to get one, too."

I must have a nose job, I think. I cannot imagine why I've waited this long. Damn, my life half over and still with this nose!

I am pretty but my nose is not. There's a bump on the bridge and too much flesh at the tip. Perhaps I'm overly sensitive about it. It hasn't held me back in my adult life. In fact, no one in my adult life seems to have noticed it. No one in my adult life has ever commented on it, not even my husband. Maybe they haven't noticed. Perhaps, after all, it was only my siblings and I who were so excruciatingly aware of my bump.

"You're getting one?" Lisa asks.

"Absolutely!"

"Your nose is like mine," Lisa agrees, rather too quickly. Instead of: "Why ever would *you* consider a nose job??" She's noticed.

"You mean, like yours used to be," I say wanly.

"Yes," says Lisa.

She goes on to tell me how it was. Not too bad. A local anesthetic, and in the middle of it, a breakthrough—she was able to really breathe.

"Yes, that's what breathing is like," her plastic surgeon told her.

And, though she only had a moment of good breathing because now her nose is swollen, she knows she'll be breathing free in another week. Her black eyes are fading now too, and the pain has gone. Also she has a date with her plastic surgeon. I ask her for his name.

"Don't get this year's nose," she cautions before saying goodbye. "What you want is your nose without the bump. You need a long dignified nose to go with long, dignified you." There are reasons apart from her looks that people adore Lisa.

I hang up and think about breathing. Do I really, truly know what it is to breathe? Once, during a physical, a doctor told me that I had a deviated septum. I didn't think much about it then, but now I do. How long have I had a deviated septum? Did I, too, have an accident or was it congenital? Is that why I snore sometimes? Is that why my nose is often stuffy? Is that the reason for the bump?

The bump has been with me for as long as I can remember. When I was an adolescent, I would stand sideways before the bathroom mirror and push the tip of my nose up with the index finger of my left hand while looking into the mirror I held in my right. My reflected profile showed a pert, upturned nose. Sandra Dee's nose. No bump. I hoped if I held it there for a while each day it would assume the shape it was destined to have.

But then one of my siblings would burst into the bathroom and catch me at it. Instead of the jugular they could go for the nose. I forgive them for it now. I see that they had to. There were a lot of us. I was the good girl, the eldest, a good student. I folded the church bulletins on Saturdays afternoons for Father O'Meara. Once I got to go to a nearby town and be my class's representative on the local radio station's quiz kid show.

Also I wasn't that nice to them. I drew an imaginary line down the middle of the bed I shared with my sister and advised her in the strongest possible terms to keep all her limbs on her side of the line. I told Mom when my brother pushed the dining room table on its side and used it as a barricade against the babysitter: me.

They needed my nose. They tormented me, first with Jimmy Durante and later with Barbra Streisand. "Hi, Pinocchio," they would singsong. And worst of all, they followed me around the house taunting me with the chant from the Alfred E. Neuman Mad Magazine record album:

> She got a nose job...she got a nose job!
> It's now turned up insteada hanging down
> She got a nose job...she got a nose job
> Now she's the prettiest gal in town!

I don't sleep all that well that night, after my conversation with Lisa. My deviated septum is giving me great difficulty. I have to breathe with my mouth open. I wonder if I'm snoring. Is it loud, constant? I think of Lisa and her beautiful new nose and I feel a pain that runs diagonally from my left nostril to the inner corner of my right eye, causing my eyelid to twitch. Also my sinuses are affected. How will my skull get air? In the morning I reach for a tissue. I have a slight nosebleed.

I roll over and face my husband. "I'm going to get a nose job." It's not easy to tell a husband of many years, one who idealizes your looks, that your nose is screwed up. Damaged goods and all. But he would catch on anyway when he saw the bruises.

He yawns, rubs his eyes, looks at me, then raises his head and supports it with his hand while he guides my chin into a profile position. "Aw, honey, I think your nose has character."

Character. He's noticed, too.

"I'm going to get a nose job," I tell my next-door neighbor when I see her in the laundry room.

"But your nose has character," she says, and proceeds to tell me how annoyed she gets when people insist that she's had a nose job when her nose is just naturally that little and cute.

"That would annoy me, too," I say, straining for empathy. I hate doing wash. Scented detergent really makes my deviated septum go crazy.

A few days later I'm at a reunion of my father's family. My Uncle Dick approaches me, kisses me, pulls away, and studies my face, clearly delighted to see me again. Then in a voice suffused with emotion says, "You look just like your mother!" I like being told I look like my mother. Other relatives have told me that this evening. My mother is a pretty woman. But then my uncle reaches up and *touches me on the bump.* "Same bump on your nose," he says, beaming, and it is almost a compliment.

This encounter with Uncle Dick should be the moment that I decide against a nose job, the moment I realize that love transcends deviated septa. But I take no comfort from it, none. Because I know that Uncle Dick is wrong, and what my mother would say to him if she were here, which she isn't, since she is long divorced from my father and all his relatives. I know, because I remember the last time our noses were compared.

The memory: my brothers and sisters and I are watching Johnny Carson on "Who Do You Trust?" My mother is nearby ironing. During a commercial my brother gets in a quick dig about my nose. For defense, I say, "I look like Mom. Everybody says so. I have the same nose as Mom."

My mother sets her iron on end for a moment and says, quite definitely, "We do not."

★　　★　　★

In a few weeks I meet Lisa for a drink. She is as vibrant and lovely as ever; her nose is perfect, and she breathes free.

"What do you think?" She flashes me a profile.

"It's beautiful. You're beautiful."

"Are you gonna do it?"

"Naw, I'm not," is all I say. Because in the time between I've lost my fervor for the fix. Call it cowardice or feminism, or both. Call me a chicken-feminist. I've decided that, while the nose job has its place, it's not on my face. This nose is mine and I am its person. It's not that bad a nose, and it doesn't breathe that badly. I will let it lead me through my days.

"Really, your nose has character," says Lisa.

Why I Dress Like
the Philosophy Nun
(1987)

I was out recently with a group of friends. "We're all wearing black," I said. We all were. All black.

"It's a New York thing," one of them replied with a shrug.

That's when I noticed it, but it's hard to say exactly when it began. Maybe when I got the black jumpsuit, a markdown at Bendel's. Or maybe it was the black ribbed knit skirt with the elastic waist band I picked up for five bucks in the United Way Thrift Shop. So I know it's been going on a long time, because I bought that skirt before my daughter was born, and now she's eight. And also because my husband recently instructed me to throw the jumpsuit the hell out.

"It's a rag, can't you see?" he asked, concern in his voice. I couldn't see. That, indeed, is the first principle of darkness. It's hard to see. The jumpsuit still looked good on, I thought, if the look weren't a close one.

But whenever it began, it's apparent that I have gone over almost entirely. It's dark in there, in the Stygian abyss of my closet. The floor is littered with black shoes: 1 pr. dress sling backs, 1 pr. plain leather pumps, black sneakers, black high tops and black waterproof boots. At this writing I count four black dresses, two black bathing suits, three black skirts, a black suit, two identical long black sweaters, (one cotton, one wool), and three pairs of black skinny pants, purchased at one time. Also a few black basque berets. To be perfectly forthright, I do own some white and beige, with an occasional splash of red at holiday time. I own maybe two print items, both gifts.

The focal point of my wardrobe is a well-loved, beautifully styled black leather jacket which I wear with everything. It has an asymmetrical closing and just the right amount of padding at the shoulders. I have never seen its peer. I am confident when I wear it because it is so truly wonderful that people have to know I went for a bundle on it. Which I did, though quite some time ago. I have gotten many compliments on it, only not lately. Lately my husband has made some disparaging remarks about its condition; remarks which leave me feeling as distressed as he says its leather is.

Now that I've accumulated all this darkness I don't shop around much. (Though I am in the market for a jumpsuit.) The black hole absorbs the shopping impulse. This is due to the fact that after a while people accept you in your black. They think: Oh, her, she's always wearing black. It can't be the *same* black. She's wearing something new in black. But really it's the same old ribbed knit skirt.

Consider male designers. Perry Ellis always wore chinos and a white shirt. He probably bought them all at once from L.L. Bean. Halston always wears his black turtleneck, and Ralph Lauren mostly wears his jean jacket. Yes, it probably *is* a Ralph Lauren jean jacket, but I still take my point: male designers do not spend their time in department stores trying on bustiers and tutus. They do not spend money buying them. They do not drag old skirts to the tailors to be hemmed for a new season.

With black everything matches. If you do carry a purse, you'll never have to change it, because it will certainly be black.

Black gives you time to think. It's what the philosophy nun said to us in college years ago. She liked wearing a habit because she could use her morning time to think about philosophy instead of making wardrobe decisions. Of course there were so many other decisions the philosophy nun was relieved of. Unlike the rest of us, she didn't have to make agonizing choices about children, men, friends, jobs, wine, plumbers, restaurants, retirement plans, and health clubs. But why not simplify life where you can? If you can't cut back on men or drink, like the philosophy nun, you can certainly wear black.

Black, furthermore, proclaims that you do think. It is not for nothing that people who wear black are thought to be sophisticated. The Webster's definition of "sophisticated": highly complicated, deprived of naiveté, worldly wise, knowing, complex, intellectually appealing. You wear it so you can think of other things, and wearing it says you do.

Also it doesn't show dirt. The other day I took one of the long sweaters to be cleaned, but only because I was brought up properly, not because it looked dirty. It didn't even show spots when scrutinized under the awesome wattage of Park East Cleaners. But I knew what I knew. Don't tell me that Halston puts on a fresh turtleneck every day.

Black tights obscure leg hair.

Black expresses one's darkness of vision. I think this is why the dwellers of our great cities wear black. It is an unconscious mourning for the people wrapped in dim blankets sleeping on their streets. Wearing pastels seems a little frivolous after what they have seen.

There's another reason I wear black. I look good in it. A lot of people do. It creates a kind of glow about the face. Rembrandt knew that.

It's like what this girl said in college. She was a senior and we were new freshmen. We were in the smoker drinking light tea with sugar. She had black coffee. We found her to be extremely worldly wise and deprived of naiveté. She took a deep drag on her cigarette, flashed us a knowing smile, and said: "Once you go black, you'll never turn back."

She was talking about something else. But it applies.

Stay Fit Forever!
Increase Your Bust!
Eliminate Cellulite!
Read This!
(1989)

We were thirteen, Carol, Barbara, and I, doing some frantic but vigorous arm circles in my basement as we chanted, "We must, we must, we must increase the bust!" It is one of my few memories of getting physical in the 1950s. Our effort had no visible effect, except for Carol. There wasn't much in the way of fitness for us children of the fifties, and even less for the girl-child. Oh yes, a phys ed class once a week, from which you could be excused if you had your period or a sniffle or a make-up test in algebra. It was before the Kennedy Administration instituted vigorous physical education programs and goals nationally. No one knew from fitness then.

Actually, try nailing down what fitness means, even now. According to the President's Council on Physical Fitness and Sports, a physically fit person is "someone who has enough energy to complete his daily tasks and enough left over for emergencies." And, from the *Britannica*, "the capability of the individual to dominate his usual environment. The degree of fitness that one requires is related to the degree of stress that he must be able to overcome."

Do these definitions mean what I think they mean? What we've always known? That life is really *really* unfair: that Imelda

Marcos, renowned chub chub, can put up her high heels and pop back Mounds bars in exile all day, secure in the knowledge that she is more physically fit than any normal crazed-out working mother who is ready to drop well before her daily tasks are anywhere near completion.

O.K. Fitness is undemocratic. It's elusive. It's anti-couch. But otherwise it makes sense. Sound mind in a sound body, all that. We know it all, but it bears repeating: most low back pain is attributable to physical deterioration, which can be *reversed* with exercise. The American Heart Association cites lack of exercise as one of the factors which predisposes a person to coronary disease. And we know that a regular fitness program not only reduces cholesterol levels, but can help stem the calcium depletion that leads to osteoporosis. Exercise has been shown to make people productive, relaxed, sounder sleepers, skinnier, sexier, and (say it!) *happier*.

"Complete fitness is composed of four factors: muscular strength, muscular endurance, cardio-respiratory endurance, and flexibility. We recommend at least three exercise sessions weekly of thirty minutes each," says Glenn Swengros, spokesman for the President's Council, and himself an author of a book on fitness. But which exercise? "Anything that you enjoy and that you can do for a lifetime. Jogging ,swimming, tennis, walking, badminton, light rowing. Pick something you'll enjoy so you'll stay with it."

I enjoy swimming and walking, but in recent years I've supplemented that with a regular calisthenics class that emphasizes stretching. The stretching relaxes me and is giving me back some of the flexibility factor I thought was irretrievably lost to the dark ages of neglect. The other day in a stretch, my forehead actually made it to my knees! I like leaving my apartment for my class. I like the quiet camaraderie with the women of various ages. I like comparing my progress with theirs.

(Surreptitiously, of course, eyeballing them, say, during a neck roll or a pelvic tilt. How does Lisa hold her back so straight? Is my leg raised as high as Cynthia's?) The emphasis is off the bust these days. I like it fine. The bust and the fitness class. Many women feel that having a fitness class provides them with a discipline they wouldn't have on their own and gives their muscles an overall workout they couldn't do themselves at home.

Ah, but in the search for a fitness class or an exercise program or health club, one must wade through a frightening murk of fitness promises. Is it possible that, as a book called *Total Fitness* (#1 Bestseller!) claims: "Even if you haven't exercised once in the last twenty years, you are only two hours away from good physical condition?" I do not think so, and I wonder who they think would think so.

And what about this ad, here in the paper, promising that if I sign on, not only will I "lose weight for life" but that I'll feel "totally revitalized" and "stay fit forever." I consider "totally revitalized" and the times of my life when I have felt even partially revitalized and the things that have made me feel that way. Actually I do not choose to discuss here the things that have made me feel that way except to say that weight loss wasn't among them. But now, staying fit *forever!* Gosh, do you think they really mean it? Terror clutches my heart as I contemplate the ramifications of such a claim.

I move on to an ad promising a "revolutionary system that restructures the body." Like cubism, maybe. Haven't *you* been needing a change, bored with the way your elbows are always there, all pointy like, in the middle of your arms? And here's one, an exercise system that will "eliminate cellulite." I call my father, the small-town doctor. "Dad, can exercise eliminate cellulite?"

"What's that?"

"Cottage cheese, Dad. You know, the dimply stuff."

"Oh that. Naw. Forget about it. You could cut it out maybe, but why would you want to?" Why indeed.

Also, what qualifications should someone have in order to lead you in an exercise regimen? Is there any kind of certifying organization? The distressing news is that in most of these United States, I could hang out a shingle and call myself a fitness trainer and be within the law. (I could teach them "We must increase the bust.") Many instructors are CPR qualified, but they don't have to be. Some claim certification from the Aerobics and Fitness Association of America, the American Aerobics Association, or The tnternational Dance and Exercise Association. These associations have impressive-sounding titles, but who certified them to certify? The most qualified people in the business are degreed physiologists, but then a lot of people out there are calling themselves physiologists. Can we really hope to have people with strong credentials teaching these classes when they often earn little more than minimum wage? Instead, what we have are goodbodies, usually very pleasant, who may or may not know something about fitness.

This is not to say that you should avoid these classes, but before starting one, you really ought to know something about fitness yourself, the most appropriate program for you, and how to tell what your own limits are. Do you know, for example, what your target heart rate should be when you exercise, and how to take your pulse?

The price of fitness varies very widely. My share (one-third) of an annual family membership at my local Y comes to $125. But if I had the wherewithal or the inclination I could be paying $1,295 for a first-year membership, plus a one-time only $500 initiation fee. But my local Y doesn't have carpet on the floors or individualized attention from physiologists and fresh clean exercise clothes every day. Its stationary bikes don't have magazine holders. I schlep my stuff when I go there. Before we begin an exercise class at the Y, we get down on our mats with paper towels to brush away the Oreo crumbs from the nursery schoolers who have used the room before us. Lying on your back doing leg lifts, you can look up to the recessed light and contemplate the crepuscular carapace of a late water-bug caught in the glass. But the place suits me. It's close, and that's very important. I wouldn't do well in a group that sported chic exercise clothes. And I'm coming to see the dead water-bug as sort of...endearing. I must, however, admit to a part of me that would thrill to my own locker with fresh exercise clothes that I hadn't washed.

Why won't some health clubs quote prices over the phone? "Each case is different," they say. "We don't know what you want." "I want to know the price of a year's membership," I tell them. What could be more straightforward? "Please come and see our facility," they whisper. "We'll talk then." Shop around plenty before enrolling. Clubs are always having specials. There are so many specials, they might think you were a chump if you went the full boat.

It might be wise to choose a place that's been around a while. My friend wrote a check for a new club and showed up for her first session with her new gym bag and leotard, only to find that the door was bolted and the proprietor...? He was probably coaching pelvic tilts in Tahiti. Certainly a new place can be very reputable, but check it out carefully.

A word, too, about a new breed that's glommed onto the scene: the home fitness instructor. You can pay $7,800 annually for fitness (not counting legwarmers) if you opt for one-on-ones with a fitness instructor who comes into your home twice a week at, say, $75 per one-hour session. (Home fitness instructors recommend bi-weekly sessions.) They'll give you reasons why people who aren't in need of physical therapy should foot this bill: "Our time is active, you don't have to wait for a locker." "I reestablish the relationship with the body." "I'm also a mime." "We have some clients who are wives of very famous men. I'm not sure I should tell you who, but —— used to be one of our clients, but now she's on the coast."

—— is, indeed, the wife of a very famous man, someone very very famous. Still, I say, if it's fame you're after, why not get the World's Most Famous Fitness Instructor, also an Oscar winner? A Jane Fonda video goes for $39.95; quite a savings from $7,800.

A WOMB OF
ONE'S OWN

The Table-top Special
(1984)

The health plan doctor suggests I have a D and C on his office table. A mini D and C is what he calls it. I jump at the chance. Off the table. Fast. I suggest you do likewise when offered this opportunity. It's an efficient little operation. It will save him time. It will save you missed days at work. Only minutes as compared to a hospital stint. It will cause you great pain. You will remember these minutes even if you've managed to forget childbirth.

"No!" I shout, as the nurse reaches for the stainless steel vacuum cleaner. "No!"

"What's the matter?"

"I won't do it, is the matter! I had it on the table six years ago!"

"But it's different. It's a soft tip now."

New. Improved. The Soft Tip. "No! I want an anesthetic!"

He is silent. He's smart. He knows that if a woman has had the table-top special once before in her life she can never be prevailed upon to do it again. Also, he knows this: that I am bleeding heavily when I'm not supposed to be bleeding at all. But one last feint. "O.K. O.K. But I'm not sure I can get you a hospital bed."

"I don't care."

He leaves to call the hospital. "I like your socks," says the nurse. "They're Perry Ellis, right?"

"Wha–?" I say. "Oh, yeah." I always wear nice socks for pelvic exams. I am in the hospital within two hours.

105

★   ★   ★

Six years ago the Park Avenue doctor said I would feel some menstrual cramps. Some? I think he meant all. All the menstrual cramps I had ever had since I was eleven. I was nauseated, trembling, and sweating. My hands shook afterward as I fumbled with my clothes. When I emerged into the waiting room the doctor offered me a shot of bourbon for my pains. Which I took. I stayed there fifteen minutes and, still faint and shaking, went out to Park Avenue to look for a cab. I stopped going to the Park Avenue doctor and switched to the health plan, figuring I could get the same pain for a lot less money. Also, he poured a crummy brand of bourbon.

So when the bleeding begins again, I know what to expect. I think I don't have a choice. Even so, I call my father, a board-certified family physician in a small town. He tells me my experience on Park Avenue was cruel and inhuman and that a D and C done in a doctor's office could never be as thorough as one done in a hospital. Don't allow anyone to do it to you again, he tells me. "What if they want to do a hysterectomy, Dad? The Park Avenue doctor told me the rule is three D and Cs, then a hysterectomy."

"That's not my rule," says my father. "We hardly ever do a hyster in these parts."

"Thanks, Dad." I put on my striped socks and go to my health plan, secure in my right to protest.

I spend two days and one night in the hospital. I eat mystery meat and tangerine Jell-O for dinner. I have a chest X-ray, blood tests, urinalysis, an enema, an electrocardiogram, an I.V. and a general anesthetic that will leave me groggy for days. What I did for pain.

A resident comes in with a clipboard and asks me to sign a release for surgery. I tell her no. She asks me why. I tell her

I'm in for a D and C — I don't want a hysterectomy. Certainly not, but she'll let me speak to my own doctor.

They have a motive for giving me a hysterectomy, I figure. I am a burden to the health plan. I have a big mouth and a womb that is wont to bleed every several years. Since I'm already in the hospital and I'll be anesthetized, they could easily put an end to my female troubles and the health plan's expenditures for them.

That night I am awakened by another resident, a male, handsome and young, who sits on the side of my bed. "You haven't signed the release for surgery."

"I don't plan to."

"Tell me what your fears are." He leans nearer. I am to be seduced into signing. But I am strong against seduction tonight. Bleeding too much, you know.

"This is a carte blanche 'to administer such medical or surgical services as they may consider necessary upon myself.' "

"That's only in the case of a life-threatening circumstance."

"It doesn't say 'life-threatening.' "

"I assure you that if your uterus is punctured, we're not going to wake you and say "Excuse me, you're bleeding to death, may we do a hysterectomy?' "

But I balk, and he agrees to wait for my own doctor. I know I'll have to sign then. Still, they'll think twice before they mess with my uterus: "That one is trouble — hysterectomy hysteric — no-frills D and C for her!"

Why do I want to hang onto the thing when I've had the only baby I want? Sentimental, I guess. I've grown accustomed to my hormones.

I lie awake. *Bleeding to death,* he said. So you really can die from D and C complications. What happens if you have it in the doctor's office and start to bleed? Or worse, if you start to bleed in the cab or the A train on the way home? What if you hemorrhage internally after, and nobody knows when you pass out in your own kitchen? These table-top specials can't be such great things, Soft Tip or no. What about a woman who has no doctor dad or education or big mouth to help her, who is bleeding without benefit of the English language or a Blue Cross card? In the name of convenience and cost control she will suffer great pain in a quick maneuver in some clinic. She could suffer more than pain.

★   ★   ★

The table-top special is one example of the progressive regression of this profession. Medical care is being rationed in this country. Titles of articles in recent issues of the *New England Journal of Medicine* indicate the concern: "Health Service Funding Cuts and the Declining Health of the Poor," "Medicine vs. Economics," "Medical Care of the Poor—A Growing Problem." The *New York Times* reports that city hospitals will receive $450 million in insurance funds disbursed by New York state as an incentive to reduce the number of hospital admissions. Sixty percent of 7,800 physicians responding to an AMA survey said that quality care had declined, or that they feared such a decline due to government interference in doctors' decisions.

In the morning my doctor visits me, wearing an air of kindly exasperation. What's the problem? No hysterectomy, I say. He sighs and assures me he doesn't want to do any more work than necessary. I sign. The nurse outside the OR tells me my doctor is a good guy, a lot of fun. He likes to sing Tina Turner songs while he operates. "Better Be Good to Me," I hum, as they put the mask over my face.

The Embryo Man
(1985)

I was nine and in Sister Dorothy's fourth-grade class in
Immaculate Conception School in a small town in western New
York when I was summoned to Sister Christopher's office.
Sister Christopher was the principal.

Immaculate Conception is important to this story, I think.
The name of my school.

I was summoned with my younger sister and brother (third
grade and first, respectively). A nurse was there, from the
hospital where my father took out babies and tonsils. The only
hospital in town. We were excused from school for the whole
morning. We were to go with the nurse, in her car, to the
hospital. We were special. We knew it.

We were so special that we were able to go past the nursery
and the maternity ward through shining swinging doors where
children could not go. Where not even ordinary adults could
go. Only nurses and doctors could go where my brother and
sister and I went that day. My father looked strange to us in
his scrub suit, but greeted us with the excitement that we knew,
the kind that only my father could bring to us. We hurried
after him. There was something amazing that he had to show
us.

It was amazing, and it is mostly my memory of it that I tell
you now, but some of it has been helped by my father's telling
of it over the years, "You remember that, Kath, don't you?"
A lady had lost her baby, my father said. She was all right,
he assured us, but he wanted to show us the baby.

109

My brother and sister and I looked at the lost baby, and were indeed amazed. It was on a towel in a surgical pan, and was no more than two inches long. "See, you can see its fingers," my father said. "You can see its pinky. And look, here . . . you can see that it's a boy. It's alive. See! It's moving!" This is where my memory fails me. Years later, he said, "You remember, Kath, it moved, didn't it?" I do not know if it moved. It may have. My father says it did. He testified before the state Legislature that it moved. He took pictures of it. I believe that he baptized it.

"The Embryo Man," we called it much later, in the congenital sickness of our humor. We laughed uneasily, but if we could put The Embryo Man in a slot with Gumby and Mr. Bill, we had control. We had him back for his hold over our childhood dreams and imaginings.

Did it move? I have tried to remember over the years. Did I see it move or did I think it moved because my father told me? And why should it be so important whether it moved or not? Because, if it moved, abortion, even an early abortion, is a mortal sin. Because, if it moved, abortion is murder.

I no longer care whether The Embryo Man moved, and I say this to my father: my father, you are father to eight daughters, more daughters than any man I know. Your daughters are women now. Because of you I am sister to more women than anyone I know, and I am the eldest of them. I have a daughter now, too. I choose all of them, women and girls. I choose them over The Embryo Man. I choose all of the women I know who have gone through the physical pain and the mental agony of their choices. None without guilt, none without torment, no matter their religion or background.

But Catholic women suffer the most. "I know I'm going to burn in hell for it," one woman told me after. She was crying, chainsmoking, distracted.

"You know it's your background," I said, to comfort her. "You wouldn't feel this guilty if you had come from a different background."

"I *know* what I've done," was all she said. I was startled by her despair and grief. She was not a practicing Catholic, and I thought that she, like me, thought of hell in metaphorical terms, if she thought of hell at all. Not so. She had been pregnant, poor, unmarried, and unemployed. She chose abortion, but believed she was damning herself for all eternity as the price.

Many years have passed since my father called us to the hospital. It is the eighties now, and I am at another Catholic school, a high school in New York City. I am to see some students there as part of a job I hold with the city Board of Education. I have been asked to wait for them in an empty office, the office of the nun in charge of extracurricular affairs. She is unknown to me, except by her name, which is on the door, and by the objects she has chosen to decorate her office: Care Bears...a plaque proclaiming "It's Lucky to Be Irish"...brochures for "Respect Life Program" and "Birthline Hotline"...greetings from a Sacred Heart family in Korea...holy water. She also has a pledge against nuclear war on her wall. I heartily approve of pledges against nuclear war.

The students are late. I glance about idly. Then I notice something extraordinary displayed on her desk. Unaccustomed as I am to messing with other people's desks, this object is so odd that I am forced to leave my seat for a closer examination.

It is a rectangle made of lucite, encasing six tiny pig-like forms. "Pig Development" the label reads, and under each little pig is its measurement: 8-10 mm., 15-20 mm., 25-30 mm., 35-40 mm., 45-50 mm., 65-70 mm. Unlike the plastic Care Bears, these forms are flesh, or were, before their mummification in lucite. They are, in fact, pig feti. Why does this nun have them on her desk, I wonder? She is in charge of extracurricular activities; she isn't the biology teacher.

They are so small, but, really, so very pig-like in their smallness...

Then I realize. I have come up against The Embryo Pig. They have been laminated to show students that from conception, there is pigness. It would be unseemly to have human feti on her desk. Far more tasteful to have pigs.

I find that I am raging at this unknown nun. It's not fair. Why not at my father? I love him, so there's that. But my father has always been a part of sex and birth and children and death and blood. He will prescribe birth control for patients requesting it. He went to my grammar school, Immaculate Conception, and is a product of the system. This nun *is* the system. She has set herself apart from a sex life and all its connections, all of its pains and joys, but will advise these girls on how to run theirs. Said advice being: abstain. And call the Birthline Hotline if things get too hot. To this end she is willing to go to the extreme of keeping pig feti on her desk.

I go out into sunshine at the same time the students leave for the day. The girls from the school are lovely, and have gotten even lovelier in the five minutes since dismissal. Some are wearing heels with their knee socks. Almost all have shortened their plaid uniform skirts by rolling them up at the waist. Some have turned up white collars and unbuttoned an extra button or two. Many have managed to apply a smudge of eyeshadow. They are out in the day in all the vitality and innocence and sensuality of their sixteen years. It's so hard to keep a good thing down!

I choose life. I choose these girls.

Having a Baby
for Pat Robertson
(1988)

I sat down and wrote this piece during the presidential campaign of 1988, just as soon as I heard that Pat Robertson wanted me to have more babies. By the time I'd finished, the next day or so, the Reverend Robertson was a loser and I couldn't peddle my essay. He and it were old news.

I print it here, though, because I believe the spirit of the reverend's proprietary attitude toward wombs lives on in our current administration. And, while it's flattering to think that women have something that men envy and want so much, I am very worried. I believe that there will always be men in power who want to get ahold of women's innards. The most chilling recent example is the late Mr. Ceausescu of Romania.

Ceausescu wanted women to have more babies because he thought it would be nice to have a bigger Rumania, i.e., more people to kill and dictate to. He banned abortions, made contraception illegal, and ordered that Rumanian women of childbearing age have five children each. There were weekly pregnancy checks in factories. Extensive maternal deaths ensued. There were many abandoned children, hundreds of orphans. At the fall of his regime in Bucharest alone, there were 20,000 women in hospitals being treated for botched abortions. An additional 10,000 were waiting for hospital beds.

So, when a guy comes along and starts talking how many babies women should have, or shouldn't have, we probably ought to take him seriously.

113

Pat Robertson, the Republican presidential hopeful, says Americans are having too few babies, that we need to encourage the birth of more American children in order to pay future bills. He says that by the year 2020 we're not going to have enough money to take care of all the retirees.

And here I didn't think we had enough money right now to take care of all the babies. This news affects me personally since I hope, with luck, to be a retiree in 2020. I thank Pat Robertson for making me stop and consider, really, for the first time: what will my retirement be like?

Naturally I'd like to have a comfortable retirement, to be able to afford a quart of decent Scotch now and again, to buy an annual pair of running shoes, to kiss the hub goodbye of an evening and enjoy a modest meal out with my women friends. But Pat Robertson has made me see things differently. He has given me 20/20 vision.

Who will pay my bills? I, who have only one child. I cannot even ask her this. I cannot bring myself to sit my daughter down and ask her whether she'll agree to pay my bills and her father's bills in 2020. (He likes SportsChannel and good coffee.) I cannot ask her, for she is only eight years old. It is too great a burden to bear through elementary school. She is happy now, a good student. Last week she won the Super Speller award for 3-212. I want her to do well so that she can pay the bills in 2020. Asking her will affect her performance now and her buying power later. No, I must have more children. I once thought she was everything, but she is not enough.

And now I look at these women friends I'll want to go out to dinner with in 2020, and I think: WHY? Why would I even want to spend time with people so heedless, so unaware? Here these women are, in their late thirties, early forties — some of them don't have any children at all, and many of these with

no plans or even husbands to get children with! They're going along, just blindly working jobs and contributing to Social
Security and pension funds and money markets in the naive
belief that this will do them. Some of them are so shortsighted
as to think that they can't *afford* more than one or two children!
They merely look at the next couple of decades and wonder
how would they support a kid, failing to see the big picture.

I know a few women now in their sixties and seventies who
have had large families. They sigh when a visitor congratulates
them on their large families and their happy retirements. They
don't seem, actually, to be retired. Either they're out working,
or they're working hard at home, caring for children, grown
children, who *will not leave!* Or children who have left and
come back because it's hard out there and rents are impossible.
These women roll their eyes and laugh heartily at a visitor's
optimism regarding their children's contributions to Social
Security. Indeed, some say they are contributing to their
children! But probably these women are the exceptions.

We have to have more children, a whole lot of children! Men
can't do it. Not even Pat Robertson can do it. He can only
preach and impregnate. But even there his position as a
presidential candidate and man of God means that he must
limit his impregnations to only one woman. (Q: How many
kids does he have?) We women have to do it, and a lot of us
better do it quickly, before menopause hits.

I briefly considered the possibility of adoption. This could
take the pressure off. Even postmenopausal women, even *men*,
could adopt six or seven or ten children now or later, no rush,
just sometime in the next twenty years, so that these children
would be wage-earner age by 2020. We could adopt needy
children, maybe orphaned children from third world countries
plagued by malnutrition and famine and war. This may be
a good idea for all concerned. Our bodies wouldn't be so

ravaged by childbearing that we'd be dead or otherwise unable to enjoy 2020, and these children wouldn't starve. They would become solid U.S. citizens, gainfully employed by 2020, happy to support their adoptive retired parents.

But maybe the wholesale adoption of third world children isn't what Mr. Robertson had in mind when he said that without a higher birth rate Western nations would be extremely vulnerable to threats from other ideologies: "We will no longer have any dominance in the world, but our culture and our values will at that point be squeezed out by many other conflicting ideologies, by other national interests. This means what we'll be as a nation, extremely vulnerable as well as our allies in Europe." I guess we should concentate on European orphans.

Mr. Robertson generously suggests tax deductions of up to $4,000 per child for people who bring their children up to be lawful God-fearing citizens of America "instead of giving money to people who might not necessarily be the productive sector." (Who are these slugs anyway? And isn't producing children productive?)

In the spirit of his generosity I request, before I start having children, that at birth each of my children be awarded a warranty to air rights over existing condominiums so that there'll be someplace to go when they reach *their* majority in a world of dwindling resources. That way we'll have them all out of our home and we'll really be able to enjoy retirement.

Mercantile Moms
(1987)

NOTE: *I am rather cavalier about prostitution here, ruthlessly exploiting it to be funny and make my point. I walk past prostitutes each morning when I take my daughter to school. They stand shivering on 11th and Third beneath a handpainted sign that says "Hookers" in a red circle with a red line slashed across the word. They are poor skinny girls who are still in their teens or barely out of them, unkempt and uncared for. They will probably be dead in a few years. How can they escape contracting AIDS in this city? No woman, really, would choose prostitution.*

★   ★   ★

ANOTHER NOTE: *If Mercantile Moms were in business at this writing, it would be offering each Mom over a million dollars for her services. This takes into account the rate of inflation over the last three years.*

I'm starting Mercantile Moms, the first feminist surrogate mother agency. I am moved to action by this sad example of yet another male-dominated profession in which women's bodies are for hire in the service of men. (Make no mistake: though some have defined a surrogate mother as one who bears a child for a woman who cannot bear children herself, a woman who rents out her womb is carrying on a man's bloodlines, not another woman's.) We women must take control of the means of production. It's a daring idea, and one that easily lends itself to politically correct franchises.

The only thing is, I'm having difficulty with staffing. I call a friend for lunch. She'd be the dream surrogate: very attractive, very smart, and experienced, having had two kids of her own. If I can recruit her, I'll be able to entice other women with dynamite genes. "How much would I have to pay you to lure you away [she's a VP at a large insurance firm] and get you on board here at Mercantile Moms?"

"No way," she says. "I'd never be a surrogate. Never."

"Come on, be open-minded. Name your price. How can you say 'never'? I mean, you'd be a surrogate, wouldn't you, if you didn't have an education, didn't have a job, if you and your kids were going hungry, and you were offered some money? You'd do it then, wouldn't you?"

"You mean if I were totally bereft, without any resources?"

"Well, yes. I suppose that's what I mean."

"In that case I'd much rather be a prostitute. You have to be pregnant if you're a surrogate. Remember being pregnant?" I nod my head. She continues, "You have to go through childbirth. Remember childbirth?" I nod, rather more emphatically this time. "And then, you have to give up your baby. I mean, I don't *want* another baby, but if I had one, I'd want to keep it. Prostitution has got to be a whole lot easier."

My friend has reason, which is why I picked her in the first place. I redouble my efforts, though, and appeal now to her humanitarian instincts. I speak of the sadness of infertility and the need for people to continue their lineage.

She remains unmoved, sipping her coffee. "Are you going to do it?" she asks.

I tell her heck no. I remind her that I'm the founder. In a little while she asks if Mercantile Moms is going to pick up lunch. "I'll get back to you," I say, and make meaningful eye contact when we part.

In the days that follow I have similar responses from other potential recruits. Basically, the bind is this: these women have either had children or they haven't; either they know all about pregnancy and so are going to be real tough to convince to do it again; or they don't, and would be willing to get pregnant only to have a child for themselves.

Perhaps if I make a firm salary offer. What would be fair? I've heard that it costs about $30,000 to buy a parking space in a Brooklyn garage, so there's that. Surrogacy does have its garaging aspect, but, of course, there's so much more to it.

My friend's mention of prostitution has given me an idea. What's the going rate for call girls — pedigreed prostitutes — these days? How do you call them to find out? "Prostitution" is not a category in the Yellow Pages. Flipping through, though, I see a heading called "Escort Services," under which run ads claiming "carefully selected sophisticated models will present personalized services . . ." and "our personalized service for *All* your social and promotional needs." They have names like "Elle" and "Tryst." Hmmm . . .

The first few I call have answering machines, but one has a real person picking up the phone. I ask her how much for one of their attractive language-interpreter VIP hostesses, thinking that a woman who has a combination of good looks, language-interpreting skills, and VIP qualities will certainly fall in the good gene pool and be right for comparison purposes.

The reply: "$500 for the first hour and a half, and $200 dollars for each hour and a half after that." Wow! Interpreting is more lucrative than I thought. I have a friend who's translated a number of books. I had no idea she was doing so well.

I thank the woman from the escort agency and hang up, in a fire to begin my tabulations.

Mercantile Moms guarantees parity of pay with any escort service. Although our Moms won't be expected to translate, there are other things to consider, among them:

—body depreciation

—loss of services to oneself (and perhaps others) in the last trimester (and in the first if a Mom suffers from morning sickness)

—insurance against the real possibility of physical complications

—the fact that our Moms sign away any royalties from baby's future production

—intensive psychiatric care to cope with the dark combination of postpartum/post-baby syndrome

—provision for early retirement. Like pro football players, our Moms can only do this job for a few years before their bodies become too ravaged or, unlike pro football players, menopause hits.

There are a lot of hour-and-a-halves in the forty weeks of the human gestation period, 4,480 to be precise. That comes to $896,300. Sounds right. I dial my friend's number. She's still not interested, but she's glad I've hit on a minimum wage.

The Holy Condom
(1987)

Even though it's all about birthing babies, a traditionally feminine activity, the Vatican's edict of March 11, 1987, "Instruction on Respect for Human Life in Its Origin and on the Dignity of Procreation," which forbids artificial insemination, doesn't consult one real woman in all its forty pages. Actually the only woman referred to by Cardinal Ratzinger and Archbishop Bovonne is Holy Mother Church, as in:

> The Church's intervention in this field [procreation]
> is inspired also by the love which she owes to man,
> helping him to recognize and respect his rights and duties.

(The church is a girl, in the same way boats are and hurricanes used to be. It's confusing, isn't it, the way they blame this stuff on a woman, when really it's all men?) Men, however, are quoted and referred to throughout, from the very first sentence:

> The gift of life which God the Creator and Father has
> entrusted to man calls him to appreciate the inestimable
> value of what he has been given.

There are three words that recur with about the same frequency as the male pronoun: dignity, natural, artificial.

The Vatican now says that sex is natural. Within marriage. It used to be sex was only for having children. If you had fun doing it, it couldn't be helped, but it wasn't recommended. Then the Church recognized what it calls the unitive function

121

of sex, and said that pleasure was O.K. too, if you were married. It was an important concession because it allowed a husband and wife to do it all month long without guilt and without contraception. The new edict has taken it a step further by saying that sex, the actual act, is the only way to conceive.

You'd think that the Vatican would welcome artificial means of conception because it could ultimately free everyone from having sex, make procreation purer. Because, even with the unitive function, sex can't be all that great if the men in charge don't indulge, and forbid their clergy to.

It is unnatural and therefore a sin to use artificial means to fertilize a woman's egg with her husband's sperm because the masturbation that precedes it is unnatural. Please note that we're talking about the husband's sperm only here. Anyone else's sperm is unnatural, artificial, and undignified. So if your husband is infertile, do something else right now. Watch television or something. Or go ahead, have sex with him. Just do not consider having a child.

But all is not lost. Catholic medical authorities have suggested an antimasturbatory sperm-collection method! During sex, use a condom deliberately pierced with a hole or two. (These holes are actually loopholes, because an intact condom is a contraceptive and therefore artificial.) There will be plenty of sperm left, and the couple can, with a clear conscience use it for insemination because it was produced naturally, during intercourse.

Rev. John Connery of Loyola, a priest and medical ethics consultant for Catholic hospitals, has another suggestion. "If a couple, let's say, had intercourse, and the doctor then took a syringe and went into the vagina and got the sperm and then injected it farther into the uterus or the Fallopian tube—if that could be done, I think you could justify it." Question, to Father Connery: Where is the doctor during the act? In the room?

Just waiting outside? If you had to stand up and take a cab to the doctor's office you'd lose a lot of sperm. Is the proximity of the doctor and the syringe during intercourse all that natural? Wouldn't masturbation have more dignity?

What if the wife waits until her husband is asleep, then sits close by him and reads something really sexy aloud. Maybe he'll have a wet dream! And then she can quick, collect the sperm and shoot it in. Wet dreams aren't a sin because they're unconscious. She wouldn't tell him in advance, so how could he know? And it wouldn't be the wife's fault. She was only reading. Reading trash is only a venial sin, not mortal. Not way up there with masturbation. Anyway, it's worth a shot.

But why is masturbation so terrible, when Ratzinger and Bovone get to do it? This tract they've written is replete with self-reference, including sixty footnotes, citing only Popes and no scientists. The Vatican's entire argument is based on things the Vatican has said before. How come I wasn't allowed to do that in my high school term papers?

Abortion is unnatural...masturbation...birth control, and now artificial insemination. I do not think the Church should limit itself to matters sexual in its vigilance against the unnatural. There are so many other things that are unnatural:
Penicillin
Indoor Plumbing
Racism and sexism
Clipping one's toenails
Starvation
Blood transfusions (If you can't have sperm that isn't your spouse's, you sure shouldn't have blood that isn't.)
Organ transplants
Hair dye and nose jobs and pacemakers
War
Contact lenses

Carrying a fetus conceived in rape to term

Starvation in a world stripped of its resources by over-population. For while the church is keeping people who want children from having them, it's forcing people who don't to have them. Will this world have dignity?

But anyway, I'm glad the Vatican thinks sex is natural. It must be, because a study has shown that people think about sex every sixteen seconds. What's unnatural is the suppression of one's sexuality. Take celibacy: it could cause you to get obsessed. It could cause you to think about sex even more than every sixteen seconds.

MEN AND WOMEN

The American Male,
and Mine
(1989)

*I was assigned this piece by a magazine editor who was devoting
an entire issue to The American Male of the Late Eighties. He had
a number of articles about men by men and he wanted one by a
woman, a feminist. Someone told him I was a feminist. He said
it could be angry. He liked it and bought it, but it didn't appear
in the issue on The American Male of the Late Eighties. And now
it's the Nineties. I'm glad it's appearing here.*

I've been asked to say something smart and succinct about
the American male of the late eighties. A few words in
summation...you know, do for the American male what
Hemingway did for the American female when he put these
words in the mouth of Robert Wilson, the white hunter:

*They are the hardest in the world; the hardest, the cruelest, the
most predatory and the most attractive and their men have softened
or gone to pieces nervously as they have hardened.*

Tell me Hemingway didn't mean it, he was just letting one
of his characters rant. But Wilson was the Code Hero, like
Rinaldi in *A Farewell to Arms*. Hemingway meant what Wilson
said.

This is my chance to get even for every woman out there
augmenting her breasts and shrinking her head for mankind.
For every time I've heard one of my sex called a man-hater
or ball-buster. (Such invectives are most often hurled in the
vicinity of a kitchen sink.) For every time I've had to pass a

127

construction gang on lunch hour. For the pornography my daughter sees when she buys her Archies at the newstand. And, for the way Archie played Betty and Veronica off against each other. For the time I was called a cunt by a perfect stranger in a bar when I was being my usual exultant self. He maybe wanted to be doing a jig in the aisle too, but didn't have the...courage. (The band was very good.)

But mostly for the strange male thighs that have pressed against mine in buses, subways, trains, planes, waiting rooms, and theaters. Why must they sit with their legs wide open? "They're just airing their equipment," says my friend Jean, and laughs. I don't think so. I am oppressed by their high thigh entitlement. They're doing it on purpose, that being contact with my thigh. Also they want me to know about this equipment of theirs, how *endowed* they are. Don't let me get started on *endowed*.

I should tell them what to do with their thighs. I shouldn't suppress my anger. If women don't tell men when they're screwing up, how can men change? But when I begin to, I am beset by doubt. Maybe the seat really is too small. Am I so irresistible that every man is dying to thigh me? He might give me an askance glance that says: "Wha? This crazy bitch thinks she's Madonna!" (And in fact, I'm not as young as I used to be.)

What if he really is some poor slob of a commuter who's had a bad day and is going home to be a good family man and hasn't given a thought to oppressing me? Wouldn't it seem a little...neurotic, if I told him, a little equipment-busting? If I say, "Scoot over, sir," he won't like it or me, and one truth about American men: they're almost all bigger than me. One truth about me: I do want them to like me.

A sentence to capsulize the American guy...I'll strive for something flowing and Hemingwayesque, a long and simple sentence which will unite the words "whiny," "macho," "big

babies," "biceps," and "noncommital" by use of that non-
directional conjunction "and."

Writing well is the best revenge. But that's the problem. Rule
#12 of the writer's Bible, Strunk and White's, *The Elements of
Style*: "Prefer the specific to the general...deal in particulars."
Where was Hemingway's famous bullshit detector when he
wrote that sentence? He was known for nailing down the telling
detail, but apparently lost it when he started in on women.
Here, take me. I'm an American woman. Am I cruel?
Predatory? Attractive? Well, O.K., that maybe, but I'm not
all those other things, and I'll prove it. Because right now I
have a chance to go for the jugular and I won't take it. Why?
Because I do want to write well, and I just haven't got the equipment Hemingway had to write a generalization like that. Say
it: now the cunt is competing with Hemingway!

Strunk and White's rule makes my job tough. I've got to
search for a specific American male who somehow exemplifies
them all. Where is he? My single friends are no help. They
report they've hardly seen one lately. We know the
demographics: only 79,726,000 men to 87,361,000 women in
the United States, 7,635,000 more women than men. There
are reasons apart from our mothers' chromosomes for the
depressing dearth. A lot of men are truly invisible. There are
500,000 adult men incarcerated in these United States, nearly
half of them black men. A Legal Aid lawyer from New York
City, regularly in the jails, tells of "lines of powerfully built
men walking two by two like schoolchildren." Countless men
are on the streets. There's no way of telling just how many.
The Coalition for the Homeless reports two to three million
people homeless nationwide. Many are, of course, women and
children, but of the people actually living on the streets, who
never find their way to public shelters or relatives' homes, the
Coalition reports that the large majority are men. Can we say,

for argument's sake, that there are two million men in our nation who are without shelter?

Many men are dead or dying. The 58,000 names on the Vietnam Veterans' Memorial in Washington are almost exclusively men's names; men who would be in their prime in the late eighties, dead now for years. That doesn't count the 2,477 men missing at war's end. It doesn't count my brother Paul, who suffered from post-Vietnam stress and died tragically on a June evening near my mother's home, with springtime and peace all around him. Paul would have turned forty this year. The newspaper called him a drifter. How many of our brothers are like Paul? At this writing the Center for Disease Control reports that 63,873 men in the United States have been diagnosed with AIDS since 1981. Of that number 24,450 have already died. These statistics add up to 2,624,350 invisible men, 2,624,350 men tragically lost to society, themselves, and the arms of women. This, without considering hard evidence which shows that men get murdered, commit suicide, abuse drugs and alcohol, and contract deadly diseases at a significantly higher rate than women and die on an average ten years earlier. Hard indeed.

Why?

Why?

You tell me this is too depressing and I quite agree. I'll change my tack and stick with American men who are alive. Who will be their representative? The Midwest farmer dogged by debt and drought? The divorced father, not the child-support shirker (damn his hide!) but the one who struggles to be a good weekend dad in the face of the reality, which is that his kids want to be at home with their friends and bikes? Is it the male at mid-life crisis advertising in the backs of magazines for much younger women who won't ask questions, women he can lure and control with money and power? What about the migrant worker with his green card, or doesn't he count? The athlete at the top of his form—what about this Lawrence Taylor person? (Oh, never mind.) I know, the successful Wall Street yuppie, singleminded and smug, exemplified by bond trader Sherman McCoy in Tom Wolfe's *Bonfire of the Vanities*. But after Black Monday, I'm not sure smug is an adjective that applies, even to yuppies.

Frustration at every turn. But wait! I see one, an American male. He's not Hemingway's Man; he's mine. He's sitting in my living room, where he has been with some regularity for the last twenty years. He is, you could say, my particular American male of the late eighties, though also of the late sixties and seventies. A writer should write what she knows, and sometimes I think I know him. He's twirling his hair. He twirls his hair a lot because he's under pressure at work. He's watching a ball game. He has nonspecific allergies, maybe due to stress. When I have a bad day, I unload it all on him and then I feel better. He keeps his bad days to himself, not wanting to bother me or upset me. We both agree that what I do, writing, is more interesting than what he does, even though he goes out into the world and I stay here in my room. In fact, I do not understand what he does and am not much interested in it except as it relates to him.

He has recently begun to go to the grocery store to buy bananas and seltzer. He does dishes these days without telling me that hot soapy water makes his hair greasy. (I say it's the twirling.) And now here comes the man's daughter, age nine. He is smiling broadly. The television is off now and they are together on the couch and he is reading to her about an American boy, Tom Sawyer. They are laughing at Tom's "grotesque foolishness" as he attempts to balance a straw on his nose to impress Becky Thatcher.

When I see him with our child, I know something about the depths of my misunderstanding and mistrust. It is a telling detail, telling about an American woman, me. It has taken me these twenty years to believe him, to believe that such an attractive man would want to stay with his wife, to believe that he could really love a daughter.

For James Baldwin

(December 2, 1987)

Last month I taught "Sonny's Blues," a short story by James Baldwin, to my College English class. It's in *The Norton Introduction to Literature*, the text I use. There is a teacher's guide that goes with this text, crib notes for professors. I have the Fourth Edition of this guide, published in 1986. Here is some of the advice it gives about the teaching of "Sonny's Blues": "Students from Harlem will know...white students from wherever will recognize and will usually at least try to empathize with this story of black experience....Is it aimed at whites...? Is it aimed at blacks...?" The guide goes on to say it is a fine story, not limited to racial issues. So then why does it suggest it might be taught in a group of stories by blacks or in a group of stories about blacks?

And why did one of Baldwin's obituaries this week carry the headline, "James Baldwin, Eloquent Writer In Behalf of Civil Rights, Is Dead"? James Baldwin was an eloquent writer. Period. It was, in part, just this sort of condescension that made him leave his country, and this city of his birth, for France, and left him feeling like a "commuter" in the world.

When I taught the story, I taught it all by itself, on the premise that Baldwin had probably aimed it at people. Straight at their hearts. And my students recognized it viscerally, the way all good writing can be recognized. There is no question of trying to empathize, no *will* at all; the reader is bound by the passion and power of the prose.

"Sonny's Blues" was written in 1965, before most of my students were born. Its narrator is a school teacher, a family man who is struggling to understand and help his younger brother Sonny, an addict. But the elder brother begins to find this understanding only after going through the pain of his little daughter's death. It is also the story of how Sonny decides to be a musician at whatever cost, because that's all he ever wanted to be. The two men are black, yes, and the place is Harlem, with its "vivid killing streets...encircled by disaster." The fact of their blackness is intrinsic to much of the story, to much of what befalls Sonny. But these men are real men and their concerns touch us deeply.

My class is your normal New York City mix. Several of the students are immigrants: from Africa, the Caribbean, Greece, Iran, China. Others are native-born blacks, Italians, Jews, Puerto Ricans, Irish. We discussed "Sonny's Blues" animatedly for an hour and a half. We discussed its themes and symbols and metaphors; racism, religion, sibling rivalry and responsibility, life, death, and the redeeming possibilities of art. As I was gathering up my papers, I looked up to find that there were four students at my desk. I assumed they were there to talk about their marks or complain about their homework assignment. But no. Each had come up separately with something more to say about "Sonny's Blues." When I left fifteen minutes later these students were still talking.

I suppose I'm an unusual person to be writing a eulogy for Baldwin. I'm a white, middle-class, married woman, a generation younger. But that may be the point.

His body is back in New York today for his funeral at St. John the Divine. My class meets this afternoon. We're doing a play from our *Norton* text, by another eloquent writer. I thought I'd lift a few words from him: "Now cracks a noble heart./ Good night, sweet prince/And flights of angels sing thee to thy rest!"

Jeanne Robert Foster
(1987)

Her name was Jeanne Robert Foster. But she was born Julie Olivier in the tiny Adirondack lumber town of Johnsburgh, New York, in 1884. And when she modeled for *Vanity Fair* at sixteen in 1900, she used the name Jean Elspeth. But when the magician wrote a sonnet to her, he gave her the name "Hilarion."

Ford Madox Ford, in his memoirs, called her "a ravishingly beautiful lady." *Vanity Fair*, in its two-page spread of photos on her, called her "unquestionably the loveliest woman ever." Her sometime lover, Aleister Crowley, the writer and satyr who practiced black magic and who was himself once called "the wickedest man in England," said she was "ideally beautiful beyond my dearest dream," and that "her speech is starred with spirituality." She donated all of the letters Ezra Pound wrote to her to the Houghton Library at Harvard.

Brancusi made dinner for her with four wines, kissed her arms in his kitchen, and gave her his prettiest plate for dessert. James Joyce gave her a recipe for Italian-style artichokes and a never-published racy limerick. In a two-day period during a trip to Paris in 1921, she lunched with Pound, had dinner with Brancusi, and, the next night, ate dinner with Picasso at a riverside restaurant in Fountainbleau.

The great love of her life was John Quinn, a wealthy New York corporate lawyer and artist manqué whose defense of *Ulysses* enabled it to be published in the United States. John Quinn owned the original manuscripts of *Ulysses* and "The Wasteland" and, in addition, the largest and greatest single

135

collection of modern European art of the twentieth century. He was already dying when she met him in 1918, and because of an intestinal operation, had to wear a support girdle until his death in 1924. Still, she wrote in 1962, "I was thankful that my hair was long and golden and that my teeth were my own until John left me." After a day with Jeanne in Paris (where they had gone to acquire art), John Quinn wrote, "This is the happiest day of my life for the last 18 years. Its story cannot be written yet. She is beauty and perfection. I adore her."

But this love affair was not without its complications, since John Quinn kept a mistress, Dorothea Coates, whom the *New York Times* called his protegée, but who claimed she was for twenty-five years "his legal wife in the eyes of man and God." Toward the end of his life Miss Coates came to be a strain on his nerves; he sent her to Europe so he could have some peace. (And so he could be alone with Jeanne?) Dorothea wrote him from the Bay of Naples: "I am looking at Vesuvius. Vesuvius is looking at me. Both of us are burning."

In her diary from 1922 Jeanne writes, "J.Q. met me. We talked of Miss Coates. The old torture begins. How can I endure the situation? There is a jealousy of the soul, a jealousy of the mind, a jealousy of the flesh. Mine is of the flesh."

But Jeanne believed in reincarnation and consoled herself with the thought that she and John would meet in another life, as they had in the past: "... a thousand years since we met in Brittany when he was Yves Iteloury of Trequier, the lawyer saint of Brittany, and when I was his serving maid who watched over him."

One of Jeanne's best friends was John Butler Yeats, the portrait artist and father to William Butler Yeats, who left Ireland and spent the last several years of his life in New York City. The old man was a great conversationalist and held court nightly at his pension, the Petipas, on West 29th Street. Artists and writers, among them George Bellows, Robert Henri, John Sloan, Conrad Aiken, Van Wyck Brooks, Rockwell Kent, Frank Harris, and Ezra Pound, came to Petipas night after night to listen to him. Jeanne had a place next to Yeats at the head table. When he died in his humble room at Petipas, there was an incomplete sketch of her on his easel. She buried him in her family plot in the Adirondacks because his children didn't have the money to bring Papa home to Ireland. She wrote a letter of consolation to William Butler Yeats, telling him that the land around his father's grave reminded her of Sligo.

Years later, in 1970, her body was buried between her husband's and John Butler Yeats's. One can view the site today in the small town of Chestertown, near Lake George.

She had a husband. One forgets this fact, since the man is rarely mentioned in her writings. His name was Matlack Foster, a friend of her family, a man older than her father. We know that he was an invalid, but little else about him. What malady had made him an invalid, and what care did he require? What did he do the three nights a week Jeanne spent at Petipas? Where was he when she was in Europe with Quinn? (In one letter to Quinn, she said only, "I'll arrange things at home.") She mentioned her marriage in a newspaper interview: "I was married on my seventeenth birthday and I think it was about then that I really began to interest myself in literary work." It was not until she was seventeen (sixteen?) either, that she first glimpsed a city, and that city was New York.

At first one thinks that Matlack Foster might have been wealthy, and that he was the means for her escape from her mountain town. But one source states that he depended on *her* for support. How is this possible? Was she able to make that much money modeling and acting? And how did she get established in a modeling career so quickly? Also, she seems to have left him, with his consent, to live in Boston for a time and take courses at Harvard and Radcliffe. Who supported the two of them then? And if she left him at that time, why did she feel the need to take him along with her to California when she went off on a fling with Crowley, the cruel, mad magician?

This was in 1916, pre-Quinn. She hoped to learn the secrets of magic from Crowley, but there was certainly another magic that he worked upon her, for she once wrote Crowley a sonnet called "Wife to Husband," expressing her distress at his earlier marriage. Although William Butler Yeats called him a "quite unspeakable person," Crowley had great magnetism and ambition.

Where did they go in California, and for how long? And how did they get there? Did Matlack and Jeanne and Crowley take the same train? It ended badly, we know. Crowley became furious when she refused to have his child. He sent her husband anonymous letters saying she was living with a lawyer and that she planned to poison him. He announced that C. Standfield Jones, an actual man, and fully grown, was the mystical child of his union with Jeanne Robert Foster. He also threatened her with a knife on the streets of New York. Why would Crowley have thought an anonymous letter about an alleged affair of Jeanne's would be so damning if her husband knew all about her and Crowley? Or didn't he?

But enough about men. The reader should not think that Jeanne Robert Foster was nothing more than a ravishing beauty with a few aliases, some lovers, and a lot of famous male friends. She was indeed far more.

Her *New York Times* obituary on September 25, 1970 (which, by the way, was only 3½ inches long) describes her as "a leading figure in international literary circles from 1910 to 1930." This she certainly was. She was the literary editor of the *Review of Reviews* from about 1912 to 1922. In 1923 she accepted the

American editorship of the *Transatlantic Review*. The *Transatlantic Review* was published simultaneously in New York and Paris and was edited by Ford Madox Ford.

She was herself the author of at least three books of poems.

Neighbors of Yesterday, published in 1917, is a volume of narrative poems about people she had known as a child. She wrote of "shrewd, kindly simple people...clannish...a race apart from the dwellers in towns...life moved in a rut for them. I have tried faithfully to set down certain things that come crowding into my mind when I remember the days of my childhood in the Great North Woods." Among the people we meet in *Neighbors of Yesterday* is Mis Meegan, married just in name to her hired man, to keep him from hiring out to the neighbors. Mis Meegan speaks: "I was born hard; to me, folks meant nothing." And

> *"I went on a packet boat as far*
> *As Rome on the Erie Canal, years ago.*
> *I was almost too young to remember.*
> *Never anywhere else, though."*

Another of the neighbors is Ezra Brown, who "died on his knees praying. He had a farm on table land, and he swung the scythe and the buckwheat cradle to the meter of the Psalms of David."

Wild Apples was published in 1916 in Boston by Sherman, French. We see in this volume evidence of her strong belief in theosophy in her poem "The Flight":

> *Past God—*
> *That Presence Dire*
> *Shaped by the racial reverence of Mankind*
> *The all-deceptive Mind*

That set Him higher
Than Man within the skies
Past monstrous God—Yea past His reeling stars
His heaven's burning bars
Past the pale Heaven of Lies
I fled.

Also, her poem "Who Am I":

All that the aspiring mind can climb to see
Within the soul's unplumbed infinity
Answers me not; so, following the Spark
Naked, I face My Own Law in the dark.

Rock-Flower was published in New York in 1923 by Boni and Liveright. In it, she writes to Ezra Pound:

You—who have given me strange music,
Leave me dumb because of the voices
Crying beyond you.

There is a poem called "Reincarnation" in which the lover (Quinn?) dies and comes back to her womb. And the unabashed sensuality of "When the Bees Swarm":

Only when I hear bees humming
In a sunny summer's drouth
I am hungered for the dripping
Of new honey in my mouth.

One of the reviews of *Wild Apples* said, "This writer is bound to take first-rank among the poets of her present generation."

She did not. In fact, *Rock-Flower* is her last known book, though she lived nearly fifty years beyond it. Why?

There was a play, "Marthe," about the Adirondacks, which had several productions and won the Drama League prize in 1926 against 700 plays submitted. She also edited the letters of John Quinn after his death in preparation for their donation to the Manuscripts Division of the New York Public Library. After the 1920s she published a poem now and again, even late in her life, but her output was disappointingly meager.

She was a delegate to the Theosophical Convention in Chicago in 1907. (Did Matlack go with her? Was he a theosophist, too?) And did JRF aspire to politics as well? There is an undated newspaper clipping with her picture and the headline "Mrs. Jeanne Robert Foster Likely to Oppose Dr. Lunn for Congress." Did she run for Congress?

She was a discriminating art critic, and in 1913, the year of the watershed Armory Exhibition of Modern Art, she wrote an article for the *Review of Reviews* in defense of Cezanne, Picasso, Derain, and Seurat. It brought her a great deal of publicity and a storm of hostile criticism. She went abroad several times, with and without Quinn, to acquire art. She did not hesitate to disagree with Quinn in matters artistic, as she did in defense of Rousseau's painting, "Lion Fighting Crocodile," which Quinn didn't buy because he disliked the subject. "I told him animals were naive, not offensive...one of the few magical paintings in the world. It has birth and death and beauty."

Her happiest times were spent with Quinn, walking in the woods of New Jersey, dining out in New York or Paris, spending an evening alone with him in his apartment on Central Park West, reading aloud to each other. Say, reading the first published version of "The Wasteland" in the current *Dial*. A diary entry of a day spent with Quinn often ends with "Great happiness!" (A euphemism for sex?) But often things weren't happy with him. John Butler Yeats wrote that "when Quinn is happy, he is an angel of light," but he noted elsewhere that Quinn sat tightly coiled like a cobra ready to strike. "I have undergone tortures sometimes with him." And so had Jeanne.

Still, she worshipped him beyond all reason. Once after he made a speech, she wrote: "I have never heard more moving beauty and pure eloquence. My God—My God—this is what I love—not the faulty man, but his vision of beauty, and for that my reverence for the flesh, my kisses, my passion." And once, after seeing a gorgeous dancer at the Cosmopolitan Club, she wrote, "I have never seen a superb and beautiful woman without wanting to give her to John Quinn. Nothing has been splendid enough for him."

Why did she want to give him other women? Why such hero worship? And why did such a fascinating woman ever wish she were "some wise and beautiful woman like Maud Gonne so he will love me"?

A few years after Quinn's death, Jeanne Robert Foster bought a large house on Albany Street in Schenectady, New York, where she lived under the same roof with her husband, her mother and father, two sisters and a brother. To support them all she worked as a counselor for the Schenectady Municipal Housing Authority from 1938 to 1955. Among her other duties there she found housing for 934 families. She refers to the "continued illness" of one sister from angina pectoris, and to her family situation as "antagonistic." "One of my sisters was a bed-ridden invalid for 23 years. There were many more family calamities."

In her house on Albany Street were pictures of her friends and paintings by some of the twentieth century's greatest artists. "No one in this Philistine city knows what my things are... She was made Schenectady's first woman Patroon. "This city has given me its highest honors," she wrote to Ezra Pound in 1963, "but they are of scant comfort." Although she once wrote that she was "sorry that I have lived so long," she does acknowledge that she had done "some good" in her later years. She opened the first Golden Age Club and founded the Senior Citizens Center and led a successful campaign to get inspection of boarding houses for the aged. She gave lectures on Ezra Pound and Picasso and her other friends to the Senior Citizens of Schenectady.

She also won a few prizes for her poetry and greatly assisted scholars and authors who made their way to Schenectady to consult her when they were writing biographies of her old friends. In 1969 Union College gave her an honorary doctor of humane letters degree.

For years in Schenectady she didn't write to anyone. Then in 1956 she wrote a letter to Pound, who was in the tenth year of a twelve-year confinement at St. Elizabeth's Mental Hospital for the criminally insane in Washington: "To bring even to mind the friends and happiness of former years gave me such pain that I wrote to no one." When Pound answered her letter, she wrote that hearing from him "was like living again." And in 1963 she wrote him: "Five operations? I can hardly imagine you changed." She describes her garden on Albany Street to him: "I always plant a long row of Capuchins. You remember—Dorothy [Pound's wife] loved them. I carried her a bunch once in Paris."

Bugs, Sweat, and Tears
(1989)

Eighteen naked women are squeezed flesh to flesh inside this hovel measuring barely ten feet in diameter. A moment ago they crawled in freely, on all fours, following the path of the sun around the central altar, actually a hole in the ground which will soon hold hot lava rocks. Each of us spreads a towel at our small place on the earth. We are in the sweatlodge, the *onikare*, the Church of the Plains Indians—far humbler than any church I have known, than the cathedral where I made my last confession twenty years ago. We have come for purification, or as our spiritual leader, Eagle Bear, says, "to unload your stuff." At least these others have. After twenty years I could use purification, and would accept it if it were thrust upon me, but I am of so little faith.

Eagle Bear—Cindy Barrett—is the only one in here who has any Native American blood. The others are white and Californian. Some call this New Age, not Native American. That annoys Cindy—Pipe Bearer and Sun Dancer—who follows the strict ritual of the Lakota Nation, passed down in oral tradition for hundreds of years, surviving even the near annihilation of its people. So how, she asks, can you call it New Age? She does say that there are some "false prophets" exploiting traditions for profit. Though she doesn't seek publicity, she is glad to have the message of the sweat carried to anyone who will hear it. "I would like to see more people following a spiritual path." Indeed, it is a message that is radiating out from the Reservation. In Folsom and San Quentin inmates can choose from sweatlodge, shul, or mass. Lodges

144

can be found in backyards up and down both coasts, but particularly where the counterculture thrives.

Cindy does the sweatlodge because she had a vision to do the sweatlodge. "There's just certain ones that the spirits pick. I don't run the sweat, the spirits do. I've learned from many teachers in my life. It's what I do. Period." She doesn't ask people to join her, but they do. A skeptical friend back in New York asked me, "How do you even know Cindy Barrett is Indian? But I believe Bear is who she says she is and believes what she preaches.

Everything about her seems straight to me. She is six feet tall and lean. Her long dark-grey hair, her erect bearing, regular handsome features, thin lips in repose, the lines across her forehead, her twangy Texan accent, the way she looks at you. When I met her she was wearing clothes: old jeans, a neatly ironed cotton shirt, a wide-brimmed hat, Western boots, a man's suit jacket. I thought that she was shy. She said the sweatlodge saved her. She is a recovered alcoholic and a recovered drug addict. She told me the sweatlodge would change me completely. Even so, I liked her.

Cindy's concept of the sweat is a profoundly religious one. "It's a way of bringing people together in prayer. I send my voice and ask how we can live in balance with our brothers and sisters. We sacrifice ourselves to the heat so that our prayers are heard. We sweat out impurities that can sometimes manifest themselves in physical illness." Indeed, Cindy claims that she has seen the sweat work physical cures.

Among my many misconceptions was that I would be in some chic spa swapping sweat with Cher. No. The sweatlodge is on cleared ground in Anne's yard, selected for the privacy afforded by tall hedges. Its frame is made from twelve bent young willows. In times past, animal hides were thrown over the willows, but Cindy has made do with heavy blankets and a tarp.

"If it gets really hot, you can lie down behind me on the ground where it's cooler," whispers Sophie, a lovely grandmother of five, on my right. "There'll be room, believe me." There is an inch of ground between Sophie's buttocks and the tarp. I am appalled at this ominous suggestion that I could go so low. "Thanks," I say, and worry.

We hang strings of tobacco ties, pinches of Mail Pouch wrapped in colored cloth, on the willow. We made these offerings in our spirit house, actually Anne's studio. Each color has meaning: yellow, illumination; black, the unconscious. They are for *Tunkashila*, or *Wankan-Tanka*, the Grandfather. Cindy assures me that Grandfather is not a paternalistic God with a long white beard, but a pantheistic God, the great spirit that is in all things. Good. We women aren't doing this for some man. Also I hold out this hope: maybe the great spirit is in me, too! A natural energy shared by us all is something even I'm capable of believing.

Ten paces from the lodge, at the east, is the sacred fire where the rocks have been heating for hours. The rock bearer brings in the first seven (the sacred number) white-hot rocks, one at a time, on her pitchfork. I pull back my toes. Cindy uses an antler to place each rock in its ritural position, and Maureen, the women on my left, touches each with the peace pipe. The women express enthusiasm about the rocks and heat, as though this is what they've been waiting for. We sprinkle bits of sage and tobacco on the rocks. The spirits like the fragrance.

Then the flaps of the tarp are let down and we are in total darkness except for the glow of lava rock. It is not the sort of darkness your eyes ever adjust to. It represents our ignorance, the womb, our dark souls. Cindy throws water on the rocks, filling the air with steam heat. Steamrooms make me so claustrophobic I have to leave. This is a pitch-black muddy steamroom, and there are eighteen of us in here! Is that tarp airtight? Will we suffocate, and will we know when we start to, or will we just be dead? To put down my rising panic, I practice the Lamaze breathing method that didn't do me a damn bit of good in childbirth either.

Things are wiggling on my bare chest, in my hair! I hope I am hallucinating already, but no such luck. It's some kind of bug that can't take the heat, wimping out from the willows. I can't shriek because we must be quiet. Cindy has said that some people are "bad medicine," and she can always tell. I've come too far to be bad medicine. Pilgrimages are not easy.

I have come from New York to the town that dare not speak its name, and will not let me either. There is no sign that marks this town. The inhabitants always steal it. We can call it Hanalei without being fey, because there is a sign, "Hanalei," on the wall of the People's Community Center. It is the town on the great Western Ocean where the aging children live, where mangy dogs sun in the middle of Main Street. Mangy dogs are the sacred animals of the place, and they know it. (No, all animals are sacred here...few get eaten.) A closed storefront has yellowing posters of Arlo Guthrie and Joe Namath. Children run barefoot, ancient VW vans sport tie-dyed curtains and rainbow decals, and some people still have names like Magnolia Tree, Tidal Wave, and Moonbeam. I say "like," for they are gentle people and I must protect them. The only one I will name truly is Eagle Bear.

In the benighted lodge now, disembodied voices. The first nine people will pray, and then we get to open the flap. I hope to Tunkashila they'll be succinct! Cindy's voice first, with a general invocation, and then a younger voice, imploring Tunkashila to help her bear a humiliating job. She prays for family, friends, her sick puppy. The next woman is sobbing, praying for her little daughter, an epileptic, and for herself, because she is about to undergo a tubal ligation, a hard decision because she is very young. I hear others weeping, calling out "*a ho!*" (I am attentive) or "*o mitak' oyas'in!*" (all my relations). These two affirmations are used repeatedly and interchangeably during the sweat in the same way that "amen!" is used in a revival meeting. I do not use them.

"I need to leave," says one woman. "Me too," says another. "Me too! Me too! *A ho!*" I want to say, but don't. Unlike other pipebearers, Cindy runs a low-threat sweat, and she quickly opens the flap without any sort of judgment. It is light! There is air! I pick a dead bug off my nipple. It's gray, the sort that's under a rock when you lift it. "Just a sow bug," says Sophie. "They're wonderful for the soil and contain silica which makes plants stand up straight."

"Maybe they'll make us stand up straight too," I say. My quip gets a response from several women: "*A ho!*...*O mitak' oyas'in!*" Naturally, I am pleased.

Obscurity once again. More prayers: to hold a dying mother "in my arms, as she once held me, Tunkashila"; for a child's ear operation; for lovers, male or female, to come back, or to leave quietly ("Let her know how much we love each other"). And finally, miraculously, the first session is ended. I crouch outside in cool ocean air, soaking, muddy, naked, and gasping. Steam is rising from my back, my mouth. A man is holding a baby. Someone's mate, I am assured. As though I cared! Modesty seems such a quaint pre-sweat concept.

We crawl back. A horn of water is passed round to each of us. Cindy says to drink, then pour it over any part of our body that needs healing. I drink half and dump the rest over my head.

Fresh hot rocks, a lowered flap, a new surge of steam. (The sow bugs have gone to their martyrdom by now, and I for one salute them.) Supplicant voices, raw with pain, begin again in darkness. Prayers for friends dying of AIDS. Prayers for the other women's prayers. Prayers to give up material things. "Let my mother and father really see each other. Let them know that they have been faithful all these years so they can comfort each other now." A prayer for the animals, to be closer to them, to learn from them. A prayer to stay off alcohol and other addiction ("It has been so hard, Grandfather!") and to help counsel others against it. Prayers for rain, against nuclear weapons, and for "our green earth." Prayers to find one's path and follow it, however humble.

My fingers are numb; there's a kink in my back. Now it is my turn, the moment I have been dreading. When the pounding in my temples wasn't too bad I considered what I could say without being bad medicine, but without betraying myself. I will not say "O, *Tunkashila*," for instance. To my surprise, I begin crying as soon as I hear my voice, speaking to the women from the ground behind Sophie's backside: "I am here to learn your path. And though I cannot pray, I offer my sincere wishes for your prayers. I will never forget this experience. Being here has forced me to confront things within myself."

I don't tell them the things within: the void that I can usually cover over. My unbelief in the company of reverent believers, when I was once a reverent believer, a girl in an organdy communion dress gripping a new missal with a mother-of-pearl cover. My citric cynicism in the dulcet state of California. My vertigo driving the road here, with its stunning vistas, heartstopping precipices, and switchback turns, nothing but cliff and falling rocks on one side, fog on the other, and ocean below. They say this has to do with sex. I think it's plain scary. The road, I mean.

"A *ho*," I hear from somewhere. "A *ho, a ho!*" They approve of me! I am greatly relieved, and besides, there are only two more people who will offer prayers. Cindy is last. In addition to her own prayers, she prays for me and my family. She is so generous and genuine and I am this imposter. "Thank you," I sob, "thank you."

The flap lifts. There is the baby I had seen earlier. We laugh to behold his sweet fat face. (If you said his name was Sky Houdini, you would be close.) Also we laugh mightily to see the light and feel the air. We pass the pipe as the baby sits on Eagle Bear's naked lap and gurgles. "*Ho! A ho! O mitak'oyas'in!*"

We crawl into light, casting rejects from *Clan of the Cave Bear*: red-faced, soaking sweat, filthy and tired and happy. We embrace and deal on a feast featuring tahini and blue corn chips. Some hose down, but most pull jeans on over dirt and sweat. These women have such lovely, well-kept bodies! Some have tattoos. One has a wide swath of indelible millefleurs across one pelvis. "That's so pretty," I say, "but didn't it hurt?"

"It did, but it felt so good, know what I mean?"

"You did great!" says Cindy, giving me a bear hug. She tells me it was nearly 180 degrees, and that, what with eighteen prayers and people, it lasted three hours. "How did you like it?"

"It felt so good when we stopped," I said.

The next afternoon I fly east, to my home in the mean, yet sometimes celestial city. East is the direction of enlightenment, according to the ritual, but I fly into a gathering dark. The pilot says we're right on course. I think of Hanalei. A quart of my sweat is in its sacred soil, and a hunk of my heart with its people.

GARBAGE RECYCLING, OR DECONSTRUCTING DETRITUS

Why Playboy Rabbits Keep Their Pants On
(1985)

This piece was written in November 1985. The Empire Club had just opened. It closed in 1986. There isn't a Playboy Club anywhere in the world today. I would be happy to take credit for this phenomenon, if I could do so without also being held responsible for Hugh Hefner's recent marriage.

I got an invitation to Playboy's new Empire Club, where they've introduced the Rabbit, "for female members who believe that turnabout is hare play." This, in the same month that Virginia Slims gave us longer cigarettes. Things were looking up. Christie Hefner's in charge now, and what with the Rabbits and all, I had to see for myself what a long way we've come.

My husband was not pleased. "I can't believe you're going there," he muttered. I told him I went only in the interest of journalistic truth, and kissed him goodbye. "Those boots look like hell," he said. I was wearing black hiking boots with my basic black dress. I thought they made a statement, something like: "Back off, man, I am not a Bunny!"

I bullied my friends into going. Marie was introducing a resolution to her community planning board, but promised to meet us late. Bonnie, Merry, and I were greeted by the maître d': "Since Playboy has not traditionally been a club for women, we wish to welcome you now by waiving the preview fee of $15." His offer caused in us a moral dilemma that we solved in a matter of seconds. Shouldn't we be paying what men paid? What if the situation was reversed? Still, it would be $60 to the good. We thanked him and accepted our V.I.P. passes.

★   ★   ★

We took a table in the bar upstairs to wait for Marie. Twin males, young and handsome, in black pants, white shirts, and black vests knit with rabbit head designs came up to us. "Sorry to keep you waiting!" one said, though we had barely taken our seats. They were Rabbits, they told us.

They weren't wearing tails or ears, and they were fully clothed. "But we expected that the Rabbits would be dressed a bit more...provocatively," Bonnie said.

"The costumes are different down in the Club," was the reply. "This is a public bar. We don't wear revealing costumes up here." But women were above stairs in this public bar wearing the boned body-binding, bosom- and buttock-baring Bunny suit that has come to be a modern icon of contempt for women. The Rabbits didn't seem to note this disparity of dress. We did not point it out to them, not wanting to seem hostile when the Rabbits were being so gracious.

"It's curious," said Merry when the Rabbits went to the bar. "You see pictures of Bunnies so often, but it's shocking to see them in the flesh." It was shocking to see very young women wearing tails and ears and hobbling in three-inch heels. They smiled and we smiled back, careful to look at their faces and not at their manipulated breasts.

The twins brought our drinks. We sipped them and checked out the artifacts of the Empire: Playboy's historic covers, a picture of the Goodyear blimp signing "Hi, Hef" in lights, a shot of the Bono family in happier times — Sonny, with Cher and baby Chastity dressed in Bunny costumes. Hef's smoking jacket, Army uniform, letter sweater, pants, and bedroom slippers were displayed in separate glass cases with all the reverence the Smithsonian reserves for the First Ladies' inaugural gowns.

We were the only ones left upstairs. The maître d' approached. "You're missing the band," he said. "My friend tells me you're waiting for your escort. I'll be your escort."

"We're waiting for Marie," we said. But we decided that Marie would find us. After making a pact that we would avoid slow dances, we descended, unescorted, to catch a little Rabbit skin.

What follows is most distressing. We saw only a few men who could be called Rabbits to at least twenty Bunnies. They were extremely handsome and unfailingly pleasant. They delivered drinks promptly and without any spills. But, if you're talking male flesh, the Empire Club is no day at the beach. Or—apologies to Gertrude Stein—when you get there, there's hardly any hare bare.

Their metallic cummerbunds and long tuxedo pants seemed to fit comfortably. One wore a tuxedo jacket that exposed chest hair. Another wore a black velvet vest that exhibited his biceps. Another wore a halter-style false tuxedo front that displayed back and arms; white cuffs at his wrists. No tails or ears. Marie arrived and pronounced our Rabbit's back "very nice," but she, too, was disappointed.

The Rabbit and Bunny costumes were designed by the same person. A man. A public relations executive for the club later told me: "It can't help but be compared to the Bunny costume, but it's a new concept in itself. It will undergo its own changes. We're still working on feedback. That's not to say it will get skimpier." But the Bunny's attire has not undergone any changes since 1963, when, after her now-famous stint as a Bunny, Gloria Steinem wrote that the costume caused welts and numbness.

One report has it that Rabbits don't wear ears and tails because they are too much a trademark of the Bunny. I do not think this is the real reason. It is my opinion that the men don't wear tails and ears because they are *undignified*, and men must have their dignity. Shouldn't there be some parity of degradation among people who wait tables in the Empire Club?

We decided to enjoy ourselves anyway. It was difficult, because the sound system rendered conversation nearly impossible. Could it be turned down? Our Rabbit said he didn't have any pull. "Find out who does, and pull it!" said Marie, to our hilarity and no effect. We resorted to gesticulation. The tables are very low, and it seemed a hardship that our nice tall Rabbit had to bend so much to serve our drinks. But then I looked at the Bunnies bending to other tables and realized that they had been made low purposely.

Our pact was unnecessary. No one asked us to dance, though there were plenty of men. We were having too much fun to seem available. We danced with one another to the band's blasting tribute to Marvin Gaye. A Bunny was dancing by herself in the middle of the floor, though sometimes she appeared to be dancing with the middle-aged couple near her.

★　　★　　★

We took a tour. The ladies' room had stalls dedicated to Bobby Riggs, Norman Mailer, and "Ex-Husbands Everywhere." Each stall had eight rolls of paper, each labeled with a male name. Trifling toilet tissue tokenism. We were only somewhat amused.

Next we were in the Playboy Art Gallery, where a painting of Gloria Steinem hung, amid many renderings of the female body. "Gloria is much more attractive than that." said the Art Gallery Rabbit.

The Empire Club is good if you want to feel falsely important. Everyone is nice. It's inexpensive by midtown standards.
You can wear jeans or a cerise satin off-shoulder evening dress
with dyed cerise shoes. The clientele is racially mixed. We had
fun there, but we usually have fun.

The upstairs bar was deserted when we left. The maître d'
gave us Playboy matches and offered to get us a cab. We were
in the vestibule when Merry realized she had left a glove. She
descended as I stood in companionable silence with the maître
d', staring at six Porky Pigs on the six video monitors above
the bar. Marie and Bonnie were dancing between the doors.
I was thinking about the Empire's New Clothes. They're wearing them, but you're supposed to pretend they're not.

A Modest Proposal

For Preventing the Children of America from Being Consumed by Cabbage Patchery and for Making Them Beneficial to the Public
(1985)

*We never did send Leah Kerry off to Cabbage Patches. She sits
bowed under five years of dust with the Smurfs, the She-ra figures,
and the Pretty Ponies. (The Barbies still get taken off the shelf with
some regularity.) I read this now with the grace of the intervening
years and wonder: What therapeutic need did I have to write it?
Why the hysteria? What elemental fear did Leah Kerry inspire?
Why did she threaten me so? Could it be unresolved rage from the
time I was eight and requested a doll and my grandmother said I
was too old? Imagine? Too old at eight? Yes, yes, I think so! But
now . . . regarding this, I've found closure.*

It is a melancholy object to those who walk through the
nation's malls, dine in the nation's fast food establishments,
and fly coach through the nation's airways, when they see
everywhere the children of this great country accompanied,
each, by one . . . two . . . three Cabbage Patch dolls, or Cabbage
Patch Pretenders. One knows what one knows, what both
Saint Paul and Frankie Avalon have told us often enough:
that these children will soon put away the things of childhood,
that they will start changing their baby toys for boys.

They lined up again at Macy's this Christmas (though I didn't
hear of any helicopter drops this year, or parents flying to Berlin

for the European Connection). There will be Cabbage Patches as long as Baby Boomers supply new young children who need to adopt them.

But consider. Consider the painful ennui on faces of children a mere ten or eleven. I have seen it. It is there, even in my own household. I have seen nascent signs of boredom on the face of my six-year-old (she's precocious) as she changes Leah Kerry's unsullied diapers yet again.

A note here: we did not stand in line. Leah Kerry was foisted upon us with the best of intentions by a dear friend who was shocked to hear we had deprived our child of a ward. And a good thing too, since shortly after Leah Kerry came to live with us, we received in the mail an invitation to a Cabbage Patch party, requesting the attendance not only of the child, but the child's Cabbage Patch doll.

This is the thing with Leah Kerry or Sandra Sue or Bradley Joe. They receive party invitations. Coleco sends them birthday cards. Parents say, "Get Sandra Sue, honey," when they go calling or shopping or traveling. Cabbages are meant for high visibility. Plenty of bucks have been spent on them. One hundred fifty gets a Kid a week at wilderness camp in Maine. Others have been sent away to computer camp. Some have gotten braces. Baby Guard, Inc., provides them with life insurance. Their clothes cost $14.95 an outfit, far cheaper to buy real baby clothes on sale at K Mart (three-month size), *if* your own kid isn't too sharp and doesn't look for the Cabbage Patch insignia.

The Oath of Adoption on the Official Adoption Papers reads, "I promise to love my Cabbage Patch Kid with all my heart....I will always remember how special my Cabbage Patch Kid is to me." They came to us as individuals with names, adoption papers, fanfare, and this tuneful admonition:

They're Cabbage Patch Kids, they're one of a kind
You gotta give them all of your love.

All of your love is a tough one, but they mean it, and our children know they mean it, and they came to many of our children three full years ago, which is a lot when you're talking that kind of love. You can't just stick a Cabbage Patch on the shelf the way you can Ken, can you?

We must help this generation of children make the transition to pubescence without an epidemic of guilt and its concomitant bulimia, anorexia, religious fanaticism!

To this end I have devised a plan for the guilt-free disposal of old Cabbages which will employ, if not the prepubescents of the land, then their older brothers and sisters, who would otherwise be on the street, or worse, laboring for less than minimum at Burger King.

The Cabbages will be returned to the Patch, Cabbage Patches, to be precise, a theme park on an ex-farm in the Midwest, which could really use a good theme park right now. It will be owned and operated by a limited partnership (units available), which will license concessions for hotels, restaurants, and rides, while maintaining complete control over the chapel, mosque, synagogue, funeral home, and cemetery.

When SugarPlum died, my father told me he saw him walking down the railroad tracks with a lady dog. What kind of thing is that to tell a kid? SugarPlum hasn't been resolved for me. I'm still waiting for him to Amtrak back with his family. What outlet was I permitted for my grief? I was cheated of the knowledge that, *au fond*, is the *raison d'être* for pets, and now Cabbages. Like the T-shirt says, "Life is hard and then you die."

So don't do to your child what Daddy did to me. Tell him/her outright: "Peggy Lynn died last night, sweetie. Pack up...we're going to...Cabbage Patches!" And by all means choose a convenient time for the demise.

Cabbage Patches will permit the working through of grief in a relaxed setting: pool, bars, saunas, tennis, good eats. The funeral, in the house of worship of your choice, will be as ornate and as populated by Cabbage Patch mourners (in tiny black crepe dresses and veils or sweet little sackcloths) as your taste and bankroll permit. There will be winter weekend specials, but a stay of at least one week is recommended as a proper mourning period.

Courtesy buses will depart from each hotel on the hour for the cemetery. Limousines will be provided upon request.

The various choices of interment will be available to the mourners, though embalming will, of course be eschewed. Visitors will select from a darling display of diminutive sarcophagi and coffins of varying quality. Cremation is also a choice, in which case your child would be provided with an ossuary with a brass plate inscribed "Requiescat Cynthia Phyllis." (Cynthia Phyllis is just an example.) Burning ghats will be prepared for those of the Hindu persuasion. Though more costly, ghats are great, and may even be the economical choice if your child is possessed of a number of dolls. It's a lot less than a family plot. Consider, too, that all the doll's effects and any Koosas (Cabbage Patch animals) may be thrown on the ghat as well. A ghat is a truly sensational memory to give a son or daughter.

An alternative often overlooked by the middle class, but one peculiarly appropriate for Cabbage Patch Kids is the choice of cryogenics, whereby a doll would be frozen until a future father could pass it along to his son, or until it's worth a whole lot of money as a collectible. Humanists may wish to donate the doll for study by social scientists who will consider such questions as "What is its appeal, anyway?" In this case a child would receive a Donor Card and an invitation to a sunset ceremony honoring that day's donors. All manner of wakes and shivas will be catered by the hotels and attended by Cabbage Patch mourners. Obituaries will be printed in the daily paper, and framed copies may be ordered at the gift shop.

I must acknowledge, though it pains me, that there are children and their parents who cannot afford a trip to Cabbage Patches. These same children are more likely to be the owners of Cabbage Patch knock-offs, which, it must be also stated, cannot be buried in the hallowed ground of Cabbage Patches. The most we can do for these children is to have them mail their dolls and a nominal check to us, and we will put them in a separate knock-off cinerarium. Ashes will be sent by return mail.

Critics upbraid me for my darkness of vision, but I say this is the way to show our children that light shines through the cypress tree. A rival has suggested another way of disposal. He proposes, for a fee, to run a search for the true parents of Cabbage Patch Kids. When the true parents are found, a certificate will be sent to the home, whereupon the *adoptive parents* (are we clear here?) place the Kid in a shoebox and mail it to the true parents. No guilt, no death, no CPK hanging around forever, and for an additional fee, renewable yearly, the adoptive family will receive a monthly letter from its Kid. Good idea for a *business*, but not so good for our children. Where's the clean break? Where's the moving on?

Finally, let me nip an ugly rumor in its proverbial bud. Detractors are saying that there will be abuses, that there are plans to run a chop shop with the donor dolls and cremation candidates, sending out prothesis parts on order, parts taken from our client dolls! They say we plan to save better dolls from the crematorium for resale to collectors, or for use as extras in our mourner pool, and instead hand out urns of cigarette ashes! Indeed. Over my dead body.

I profess, in the sincerity of my heart, that I have not the least personal interest in endeavoring to promote this necessary work, having no other motive than the public good of my country, by advancing our trade, providing for infants, relieving the poor and giving some pleasure to the rich.

The Hole of '88
(1988)

Wednesday, 6:30 a.m. It begins. I do not need this hole right now. There are other things: bills, a deadline, papers to correct, a husband brought low by pollen.

It happens without portent, none of the auguries New Yorkers have come to dread. I am grateful. Yes, for I well know what it is to find that a crane or a dumpster has been moved onto one's block, ominously stationed there, waiting... waiting....

Or worse: a waiting dumpster with *a covering.* A dumpster with a covering on one's block—now, *that* is a truly heart-stopping sight. Nothing can be done about it. You can't move anywhere else. You live in Manhattan already. But you know what awful stuff is going to be dumped there, what radon dust and airborne asbestos you and your loved ones will bite back for months, if the dumpster closest to you has been provided with *a covering.*

So I am glad to be spared the psychic pain of knowing in advance. I don't get any nutty thoughts this time, like whether I should try to get my neighbors together for a human chain against the machines, or, you know, something really crazy like calling the highways division. It's a done deal and I am relieved. The street was taken swiftly and by stealth in the dead of the night, and we were permitted our sleep until now.

We wake to it on this dark morning, to the sound of exhaust from something very large and to its intermittent backup beep-beeps. So we know it's the hole. But we dare not look until we have our first fortifying sips of caffeine.

It's definitely going to be a biggie, though not like the hole of. . .'78, I think it was. That went on for blocks and blocks and lasted for months, requiring wooden footpaths. We're talking real heat and dust that summer. Right now, the length of only one block, ours, has been marked off by a dotted line painted during the night.

The machine that is cutting along the dotted line is huge and yellow and has this accessory that looks like a big pizza cutter, only it's a grinder, and right now it's grinding away at the middle lane of our avenue. Cars, surprised by the sudden detour, are honking. An ambulance wails its way to the nearby emergency room.

My child, bless her, remains asleep. She is a sweet city child. Also, she does not remember the hole of her formative years ('83, was it?. . .or '84?). Actually, though she suffered no trauma, one of her playmates had a recurring nightmare about falling into the hole. I believe this to be a pure response to the hole, occurring as it did well before Baby Jessica's plight suggested to our nation's children the attention-getting possibilities of such an act.

I go out to my day and return in the afternoon. The pizza cutter has been exchanged for a steam shovel and a dump truck. My husband isn't home. I flop down on the bed and call his office. "I thought you were too sick to go in today."

"It was so noisy."

"Oh." The bed is vibrating and it's not supposed to. (It's a platform.) I mention this.

"The flat part of the steam shovel does that when it smashes down on the concrete to break it up," he explains from the World Trade Center. "Remember?"

"Oh, yeah." I dial my friend then.

"Listen, call me back when you get home," she says.

"I am home."

"It sounds like you're on a corner someplace."

We do not know the reason for the digging. Our avenue has never been marked for a subway route. And they have never planted tulips down its center.

During the hole of '83, I stopped and asked the workmen, "Why are you digging?" Bemused by my temerity, they laughed a little among themselves. Then a representative swaggered forward and spoke.

"I lost my watch," he said. "We're lookin' for it."

In the evening I go out to the newsstand. The workmen are gone. A temporary fence has been erected from wood and Day-Glo orange plastic chicken wire. The site is marked by orange plastic traffic cones and sawhorses with orange reflectors. The crosswalk is blocked. I walk in the intersection. There isn't much traffic, so I lean against the flimsy fence and look in. By the early moon and the sodium-vapor streetlamp, I see the hole itself, still small, the hulking steam shovel, and a pile of lumber. Tomorrow, I know, the lumber will be driven in to line the hole, perhaps to keep my building and the buildings behind it and the river behind them from slipping in.

I make my purchase and quiz the vendor. Does he know why, maybe?

"No, I surely do not. But last week someone around here smelled gas, and I'd rather have the hole than gas, God forbid."

"Yes, God forbid!" I say.

Soul on Ice
(1989)

It was Girl Scout Day at the Ice Capades. Madison Square Garden was filled with Brownies and Girl Scouts and good mothers. I was instructed by my daughter, a Girl Scout-in-training, to sit several seats away from her. I did, with a dozen Brownies. There was a literal-minded Brownie behind me. She paid very close attention and sought to explain the proceedings to her friends. "They're supposed to be under the sea now." "Don't talk so much, Isabel," her friends said. "They're really not flying, they're attached to wires." "Be *quiet*, Isabel!" I identified with Isabel: intense, filled with wonder, not wanting to be conned, maddeningly naive.

There was a hush as the featured act was announced, Jill Watson and Peter Oppegard, Bronze Medalists from the 1988 Olympics. Applause, applause, applause, and then Isabel: "She's not really naked, it's just something that looks like skin."

"Shut *up*, Isabel!"

Jill Watson did look naked, but for the tatters of bright cloth stuck strategically on her second skin. Peter Oppegard didn't require any explanation. He was wearing all his clothes. Male athletes get to.

Isabel and I were both disturbed by Jill Watson's costume. She was more naked-seeming than the other women, though their costumes were also quite meager. I started thinking of the widespread use of illusion material in the women's costumes, all the flesh-colored tights and body stockings. Which made me muse again on flesh color, the way I do every time I put on a Band-Aid. And then I thought—I was at the Ice Capades,

167

after all...I had two full hours in which to think or die. I thought: the flesh color of these costumes is all the same color, like Band-Aids. It is the color of white people's flesh. Because, although there were sixty-five people (I checked later) in the cast of the Ice Capades, there was not one black person. (Though there were many black people in the audience.)

Maybe they don't know how to ice skate! That was me, not Isabel, but she was probably thinking it too or at least that would be her answer if this were pointed out to her. But wait, doesn't Harlem have its own ice-skating lake in Central Park, just like it has two basketball courts on every block?

And then there's Debi Thomas. She's a pretty good skate. Indeed, later in the weekend, Ms. Thomas, who is now pre-med at Stanford, was on television in a competition in which she did a modified striptease, taking off two small-enough layers to a teeny tiny something which left very little to illusion. I know, because my daughter recorded it, and has already watched it several times. So she knows what great athletes have to do if they're women.

After the spectacle we left Isabel and the girls at the drop-off point and made our way home. I mentioned my observations to my daughter. I don't really do this to make her crazy, though that may be the final effect. Still, if she's going to be a Scout, or a woman in this world, she should be prepared. How else can she get her The Way Things Are badge? So I say, "Did you notice that almost all the women were blonde? Did you notice that the men wore clothes and they didn't? Did you notice that there were no black people? (I had taken her to *Forty-Second Street* just before it closed. It, too, had a huge no-black cast[e]. I pointed this out to her at the time, not wanting her to think that blacks can't tap-dance.)

"Oh, Mom." A great sigh. It is not easy to be the child of socially conscious parents. "There *might* have been black people in the Ice Capades," she says. "What about the California Raisins?"

I've been meaning to get to the California Raisins. They're the most popular act in the Ice Capades. What my daughter meant was that a black person could have been supporting one of the unwieldy raisin costumes, who knew? But in fact the Raisins were the only ones on the ice who didn't have white flesh. Their faces were caricatures of black faces. And they spoke black jive street talk, the way the plant spoke in *Little Shop of Horrors*, the way the men in blackface spoke at the minstrel show I went to as a child. When they entered, to Marvin Gaye's "Heard It Through the Grapevine," there wasn't a Scout in her seat. There were seven Raisins, but only one female Raisin. (Yes, there *were* many women in the Ice Capades' cast, but that's because it's barely different from the shows that advertise 40-GIRLS-40.) This female Raisin is some kinda tough tambourine-packing mama with crazy Raisin hair piled high on her head. She puts these male Raisins in their box in short order and tells them she's gonna let them know what she wants. She then struts around the ice in a blasting Raisin-synch of Aretha Franklin's fabulous voice: R-E-S-P-E-C-T.

"R-E-S-P-E-C-T," the Girl Scouts sing, clapping and dancing in place. They are crazy for Ms. Raisin. R-E-S-P-E-C-T. . .that's what they want, too!

In fact, Ms. Raisin is a Band-Aid, there to keep girls like Isabel dancing in place. She has appropriated Aretha's talent to create an illusion not unlike the cloth used on the women's bodies. "Don't worry, be happy," she's saying. "Hey, girls, we've really got things covered!" I think the person supporting her is white. I think that he's a man.

Disney World
(1989)

I went to Disney World Post-Easter, a true Malthusian nightmare. It was a lot like standing on the IRT for four days. Summer is said to be nearly as populous, and the summer of '89 should be especially so, since May 1 marks the unveiling of the much-hyped Disney-MGM Studios Theme Park. I am here to tell you.

At first it's easy to feel elitist: thousands of boys with tendrils down their necks wearing Gitano shirts and baggies. Gum-chewing girls with feathered hair walking beside faded parents. Old people dragging along on line with the grandkids. (Are these the terms they must endure for the family to come visit them here in Florida?) Such a naked look at the American family! Until you remember you're one and you're here too. And then all you feel is pity, self- and otherwise.

We've made this pilgrimage to pin money on Mickey's icon, but we'd better quick get out of his way before he parades down Main Street. And hey, get out of the way of that major street vacuum after the parade! Because it's as inexorable as death. Disney World has got to be clean, dontcha know, and you have got to move.

There are lines everywhere for everything, culminating in an hour-long line each night for the two modes of transportation you must take to get to your cars once you've exited the Magic Kingdom. Soon you realize the lines are the thing itself. All the rest is a kind of commercial interruption. In fact, many attractions are sponsored by the likes of Kodak, General Motors, General Electric, Exxon, and you know it.

The guidebook says certain attractions are "not to be missed," but is it stuff you want your kid to see? It's a Small World has only a few really black faces among the hundreds of little robots in its world. In the Pirates of the Caribbean, women are auctioned off and chased in a brothel-like setting. Native Americans are depicted as tom-tom banging, warmongering Indians—you know, the kind that killed off all the cowboys. And can a Michael Jackson video ("Captain EO," at Epcot) really be worth a forty-five-minute wait?

No opportunity is lost for a pandering paean to patriotism or progress. The pageant on the steps of Cinderella's Castle tells us: "Walt Disney had a vision for a place where all America could come and enjoy. Y'know, at a time when lots of countries are building walls to keep people in, the United States still has people knocking on its doors." American Journeys in Tomorrowland tells us how great our farms are doing: "We feed all of our own people and much of the rest of the world besides!" The Land at Epcot rhapsodizes that we're finding ways of growing plants without soil and demonstrates by showing clamps that drag the straggly roots of a few unhappy plants through several mystery substances. A gigantic float of a flag and an eagle passes at the end of the Electric Light Parade (a half-a-million light bulbs!). And at night the Great Voice-Over tells us, "To honor America we present our grand finale, a fantasy in the sky" as red, white, and blue fireworks detonate to "This Is My Country." Like Lee Iacocca, Mickey is good for America, and America is very, very good to Mickey.

Remarkably, apart from bringing kids there in the first place, I witnessed no other incidents of child abuse. People seemed to be very loving to their children. They saved to bring them here, didn't they, to show them their love? Some people, by the look of them, saved for a long time. And knowing this, the kids were very good. Only the babies didn't understand

and wailed their protests at the claustrophobic conditions, the heat, the strangers, the exhaustion.

The crowds observe the Code of the Line. I saw only two incidents of line cutting in four days. It is bad form and un-American to complain too much about the wait. A kind of macho line bravura develops. People don't speak or laugh much. You want to be attentive, so that if any gap develops you can move quickly to fill it before being prompted. Eye contact is avoided. This is partly because eyes are glazed over, but there's something else. Although there should be a kind of bond that forms among strangers in a situation of shared degradation, it's dangerous. Because if you scratch the surface even a little, you'll get at the truth, which is: this isn't what fun is.

Big Thunder Mountain Railroad is a truly terrifying roller coaster, but not nearly so fearsome as its line. The line was made longer because, twice during our wait, the ride suffered a mysterious, unexplained "breakdown." This was the hushed word that passed from waitee to waitee. An excellent example of line mentality: very few people gave up, even though we were all waiting for a ride on a very scary malfunctioning roller coaster. One of my young companions burst into tears when it was over: "It's not *fair*! We waited over an hour and it lasted two minutes!" I was glad it was short.

You may still want to give your child this dream vacation (and there's a lot of pressure to if they haven't been in a plastic bubble since birth). A few rules:

1. Don't buy a four-day Worldpassport. That's how they get you. I paid $275 for three of us, one of whom was under 12, so damn! we had to go. Pay for one day (approximately $30 per adult—Walt doesn't get too specific about his prices) and check it out. Remember that there are other attractions in Orlando that might be less crowded and (dare I say?) more fun. Your hotel swimming pool, how 'bout? I wouldn't know, though.

2. Don't give the kids fifty bucks for spending money. Keep it and buy them presents and balloons as you go. Kids think its crazy to buy that stuff. They'll tell you they're going to save their money and buy Nintendo with it. So then you're put in this morally compromised position of telling them, *Buy the frigging Minnie ears, damn it!* But they just *won't!* And then you feel guilty because they don't have Minnie ears like American kids should and so you buy them. Really, you must buy things so that there's something to show for the experience.

3. Remember that you're not there to receive an education. Not if you read books or the *National Enquirer* on a regular basis. Because this is not what education is, either, though some think otherwise. When you catch yourself blearily straining to understand what exactly it is Mission to Mars is saying about the relative size of that Mars volcanic crater onscreen, think: *Would I be watching this if it were a documentary on Channel 13?*

4. Import PB&J sandwiches each day. Yes, I know Mickey doesn't like it, but he's not *really* omniscient and may never find out. Mickey says, "The Magic Kingdom has no picnic grounds." Note: I do not think this is the real reason you can't bring in food. If you don't, you'll be standing in a long line at Tomorrowland for what looks to be barbecued beef.

5. Free yourself from any guidebook rules that instruct you to get there at 7 a.m. (an hour before opening time), take a position at the rope barrier, and then sprint to Space Mountain! We actually entertained the possibility of a wake-up call the first morning. By day two, however, there was a lot of stalling going on. No one actually said they didn't want to go, but it took *so* long for our showers, after that there was this mean game of spit that got going. . .

6. Never take a baby since they can't be trusted.

7. If you only have two weeks off during the year, don't do it, don't do it, don't do it. Instead take the kids to *Anything*

Goes, *Oil City Symphony*, a Tiffany concert, and dinner at Lutece, Le Bernardin, and Le Cirque. With the money you save, buy Nintendo. Or, if money's tight, stay home and rent *Splash* and *Pee-wee's Big Adventure*. You'll have a lot of fun.

Why Can't Sigourney Be a Ghostbuster?
(1989)

Five years, five long years, and still no female Ghostbusters! How long must women wait to take their rightful place among them? Aren't any women qualified? Isn't there one woman out there who's be right for the job? Isn't Sigourney Weaver, even, a good enough woman? I submit that she is!

Must Ghostbusters, like firefighters, demonstrate physical prowess to get the job? But Sigourney could pass, I just know she could! Who, after all, has demonstrated more awesome strength and courage under fire? She saved the whole world in *Aliens*, not just New York City. Slime is nothing after all she's been through. And she stands as tall in her stocking feet as any of her leading men. Dan Ackroyd clearly didn't stay in training in the years between: he can't be considered at the top of his ghostbusting form. Sigourney is the ideal candidate, but look who gets the jobs. She's even passed over for Rick Moranis's wimpy weakling.

Out of nostalgia for the bygone days of affirmative action, the black Ghostbuster has been permitted to stay on the job. Of course, he's not on-screen as often as the others, and he never did get his doctorate like they did. He doesn't get to spout their wild pseudo-scientific spoof lines like "Are the strontium 90 triglicerides set to go?" No, the black Ghostbuster is relegated to street talk like "That is *some* heavy stuff!" He just doesn't seem to have mastered the nomenclature and the theory supporting the science. Also he gets scared more easily than the others. You see the fright on his face just like Buckwheat in *Little Rascals*. Tokenism leaves much to be desired, but at least he's active and on the front lines. He gets to carry a power pack and shoot ray guns, for goshsakes! What lessons can young women draw from *Ghostbusters*?

Ms. Weaver's Dana is talented, obviously. She has two desirable part-time jobs: restoring masterpieces and playing the cello in an orchestra, I think the Philharmonic. So there's that. And she must be very highly paid because her husband ran off and left her with the baby and still she manages her great clothes and that really nice baby carriage and the upkeep on an exquisite apartment. All to the good. But here we have a woman who, though highly successful, keeps on attracting bad ghosts and husbands and boyfriends! Why is she always the victim who needs to be rescued? Dana does take action at the end, braving the Evil Carpathian to save her baby boy. And she does have the strength of character to turn down his offer to make her mother of the god of the world. But this occurs late in the film and could be attributed to a simple surge of maternal hormones.

And doesn't that slime, which begins attacking her from her very own bathtub as soon as she takes off her shirt, look like a—a giant phallus? Why was she wearing a bra instead of her *Aliens* undershirt? (What does the consistency of slime remind you of, by the way?) As talented as she is, she isn't a Ghostbuster, but relegated to the roll of Angel in the House of a Ghostbuster, cleaning up Bill Murray's filthy apartment as soon as she set foot in it, never mind that she has to be crazed with worry, what with ghosts in hot pursuit of her baby boy.

Look at the other women. The ditzy Ghostbuster secretary who hobbles instead of walks. The prosecuting attorney whom Bill Murray calls "Kitten" and who suffers the greatest disdain in the movie. The ghosts carry her off upside down to her ignominious end. So much for women lawyers! And finally there's the Statue of Liberty, a woman so untainted, so pure, that she alone can bust the ghosts. They enter her. They get inside her head. They play music for her. Finally she leaves her home and walks through water to save New York. For thanks she's left flat on her back after the job is done. Seduced and abandoned!

Perhaps the producers of *Ghostbusters III* will see the error of their ways and promote Sigourney. But now that I think of it, will she take the job? When she was offered the opportunity to accompany the boys through the sewers in search of slime and cockroaches, she declined. Maybe there are some jobs women just aren't cut out for.

It's What's up Front That Counts
(1989)

You've seen the new Camel cigarette camel, haven't you? He isn't a phallic symbol, he's a phallus. Well, in case you've missed him, this is something you must know: his nose is a penis, his jowls are testes. Bigger than anybody's! We've long known that cigarettes are oral, cigarettes are phallic, smoke a cigarette and you can have a penis too. (If you want one.) But, I mean, really...

This didn't get published anywhere.

This guy I've been seeing, he used to be so stately, but he's changed his image. He's a smooth character, un tipo suave. He's hairy. He's seen at every watering hole. There are thirteen icons of him in my newstand alone. He's James Bond for the nineties. What women really want. He surfs, erects skyscrapers, plays pool, and carries a big cue. He has a yacht, a red sports car, a submarine, and a private jet. Ooooh, but thatsa not all he's got! How do you think he attracts all those Barbies? Not by humps alone. Because he'd walk a mile for them? Because he can hold his water? Because he's such a beast? Or is it that he's so dangerous he comes with a label?

No! He has what Ken never did have.

Well, it's actually kind of a deformity, isn't it? (Where it is, I mean.) Like The Elephant Man, only he's The Camel Man. And people *can* be unkind. "Doesn't he look like a dick?" a detractor wrote across his face. But it's true. He does! He really does! But most folks have such delicacy they claim never to have noticed, or, if they are repelled, remain silent.

178

He hasn't let it hold him back. Check his performance. His parent company, R.J. Nabisco, says he's turned sales of his product around since he started representing them. I did market research: "How are sales doin?" I asked at the newstand. "Great, come to think of it. We're selling 'em by the carton." So they're sure to keep him on, even though some killjoy complained that his advertising campaign sticks its dick in our faces.

I've tried to resist him, but he's put me through some changes. I saw *Lawrence of Arabia* the other night and it just wasn't the same. Like, who even looks at Omar Sharif anymore?

THINGS THAT GO
BUMP IN MY NIGHT

Insomniac Pride
(1988)

A while back, when I was going through a protracted period of insomnia, I moved a bed into the dining alcove. I squeezed the dining table between the bookshelves in the living room. When you can't sleep, you will do anything for sleep. You will choose sleep even when it means you can't throw expensive dinner parties. I, who had never thrown expensive dinner parties, now got to say, "I'd *so* love to have you over for a dinner party, but there's this bed in my dining alcove."

It was a really pretty brass-and-iron bed that I had bought at an auction for $22. It was quite big. It was the first thing people saw when they entered my apartment for reasons other than dinner parties. I went to Orchard Street and had a quilt and pillows made in a provincial print to disguise the bed. People would think it was the couch, maybe. But we already had a couch. Lumpy and wire-sprung, where a couch was supposed to be. Visitors knew it for the bed it was. "A *bed?*" they said. And oftentimes, this bed was unmade. It was so, oh . . . so un-middle-class. Would they report me to the landlord?

There are two bedrooms in my apartment, which at night were invariably occupied by sleeping people. I needed a place where I could read and obsess and toss freely about until dawn. I didn't want the hassle of opening a couch-bed . . . the noise, the threat to one's fingers and lower back, the schlepping in darkness for a blanket. I wanted a *bed*, with its own cover and pillow and light; a bed that would take me when sleep didn't. The bed set me free, a freedom that sometimes even permitted sleep. It was the beginning of my adjustment to my affliction.

183

Other things helped as well. Ironically, as distressful as those sleepless nights were, enduring them actually gave me a kind of dumb confidence. I found that I could do whatever I had to do the next day; after all, so many sleepless nights had passed, only to be followed by relatively productive days.

More important, however, was the knowledge that I couldn't begin to hallucinate from lack of REMs. You don't, you know—a *doctor* assured me. It's an evil myth, insomina-inducing in its own right, perpetrated no doubt by some smug easy-sleeper.

It's hard for isomniacs to get any sympathy, since most people think they're already awash in self-pity. They make nasty remarks such as: "Don't lose any sleep over it" or: "Why don't you check in for some shock treatments?" These remarks hurt insomniacs and cause them to stay up even later pondering peoples' purposes.

And things are even tougher for New York insomniacs. A walk outside is not a good idea. It's hard to take back the night singlehandedly. And what if you don't have a dining alcove? What if there's only one room total, two of you in it, and one of you is sleeping? New York insomniacs cannot get up and go downstairs and make a cake every night, the way one of John Cheever's Connecticut characters coped.

The table has been back in the dining alcove for some time now, ever since the occupant of the smaller bedroom outgrew her crib. In fact her growth eased my insomnia a good deal. She was once so very small that someone had to stay awake nights thinking of her vulnerability and mine, and of how she was apt to awaken at any moment. This last was wishful thinking: I wanted company.

I make do now with a wool throw on the couch, and my waking time is down to an hour, maybe two. But I am an insomniac, the way some people are Rangers fans or Lutherans, and I have come to take the same primal pride in my identity as these. For one thing: Did you ever meet a *stupid* insomniac? Did you ever meet an insensitive one? (Macbeth was a villain, but can you really say he lacked feeling?) And, in New York, with its sirens and stress and sadness, isn't insomnia, after all, the correct response?

The School That Looked Like a Castle
(1985)

The pastel sign in front of the old building on 10th Avenue runs from 58th to 59th: "A Landmark For Business...200,000 Square Feet...Unique Office, Retail and Restaurant Space." The former Haaren High School in the former neighborhood of Hell's Kitchen is coming to us next spring as — ladies and gentlemen — the all-new media facility, Metropolis!

The building is part of my life, where I first saw duty as an English teacher some seventeen years ago. Haaren came to me by default. I was new to the city then, newly graduated from my sheltered women's college. I was hired by the Board of Education and reported for my assignment to a hall where a man called out names of schools. When he did, people raised their hands. No one told me to raise my hand when he said Stuyvesant or Bronx Science. I decided, though, that I'd better act before all the jobs were given out. I raised my hand for Haaren. Mine was the only hand up.

I was twenty-two and green. By some perverse logic I, the least experienced teacher, was assigned the most experienced students in the all-boys school, potential dropouts in the work-study program. Some were eighteen and nineteen. They didn't learn much but I learned plenty. Once I came into class to find a colorless balloonlike object marking my place in *Macbeth*. I held it aloft. *"What is this?"* I imperiously asked my group of young men, though I realized even as I spoke it was a condom.

186

★   ★   ★

I was being tested, the way it happens in the movies. "Some people can take the challenge, others can't — it's that simple," the dean of students told me the first day as he fished my empty purse from a garbage can in the basement. That whole first year the dean of students was to show an uncanny talent for recovering my empty purse.

There was nothing left in it but a sanitary napkin. "I didn't look inside," said the dean hastily, so I knew he had. He gave me carfare home.

I took his challenge and stayed four years, the foundation of my life in New York. This, despite the shop teacher's warning uttered in the most ominous of tones, "Take my advice, get out of Haaren." He wasn't the only one. Robert Mitchum, its most famous son, told a talk show host that it was a finishing school: "If you went there you were finished."

In time I got tough and the criminal element moved on to an easier mark, leaving me free to grapple with my students' high absenteeism and rage, low self-esteem and reading scores. In the early seventies the student body hailed from fifty-four countries of origin by way of Harlem, the Lower East Side, Chinatown, and Astoria. What they had in common was poverty.

The faculty, too, was varied. We talked all the time in the teachers' cafeteria, heatedly debating such questions as the morality of failing boys in their last year of school in a society and system that had failed them, when poor marks would leave them even more susceptible to the draft in a time of war. I flunked a lot of them the first year, I failed fewer and fewer in the years that followed.

I was so preoccupied with my problems and my students' problems that I never noticed the building, until a shy boy from the Dominican Republic told me, "I call it the castle." The school had a look. It was beautiful, though in a sorry state of disrepair. A seven-story brick and limestone structure of a style called Flemish Renaissance, it was built in 1903 by Charles B.J. Snyder, a specialist in school architecture. Mr. Snyder generously threw in what he could for love and beauty. The facade is a glory of contoured cables, engaged Gothic columns, acanthus leaves, and charming reliefs of muses and of sweet-faced boys, their heads center-parted in the style of another age, dutifully reading their books. Mr. Snyder made large classrooms with high ceilings and many windows. When I was there the upper rooms had views of the Hudson.

Haaren had poor lighting, dingy paint, bare floors, some broken doors and windows — things a relatively small infusion of funds might have remedied. Certainly nothing like the money the developers of the Metropolis are spending. In those days teacher cabinets were coveted above all else. A place to put your stuff. I schlepped my books and coat around for months before I finally went in to the administrative assistant and tearfully demanded a teacher cabinet. Who did I think I was, he roared at me. There were teachers who had been here years, *tenured* teachers who didn't have their own teacher cabinets!

★   ★   ★

I left Haaren in 1972. Later the school merged with Food and Maritime High School to become Park West High School, situated on West 50th Street between 10th and 11th Avenues. The rationale was to combine two underpopulated schools in one, with one administration. Park West, as grim and joyless an edifice as can be found, typifies the mean-spirited new Cinderblock School of School Design. It cost the city $29 million. Low-ceilinged and boxlike, it has poor ventilation and leaks.

For a while noxious fumes from an adjacent garage pervaded the guidance area. Little could be done because, like fully half of the classrooms, the guidance area is without windows. When rooms do have windows they are often above head height, the size of basement windows. In winter some rooms are hot while others are cold. Cheap ceiling tiles are missing; the floor buckles in places. "It looks like a factory" one teacher there told me.

Mr. Snyder's castle was sold by the Public Development Corporation in 1981 for $1.5 million. Forty million dollars is now being spent on the Metropolis. Much of the original structure, architecturally and esthetically sound, will stay, and certainly its beautiful facade. But you can see sky from the spot where the auditorium once was. It has been gutted to make room for the atrium with three escalators and two thirty-foot-high waterfalls.

The two buildings in Greenwich Village that were once Food and Maritime High School are still owned by the city. One is used an an alternative school and the homeless line up for meals at the other. Why was Haaren not used for the public good?

The future clients of the building, video artists and television producers, will prosper in their surroundings, filled with sunlight and floral paintings. But as I stand on a construction walkway above the mud I can only look back. I think of my students M. Green and A. Reader, killed in separate incidents on Harlem streets before they even graduated. I think of the ones destroyed by dope. I think of the thirty-ish man I see in my neighborhood, overweight and idle — a former student. We used to exchange greetings, but now it is too painful for us, too much a reminder of hope he once had. I think of J. Il An, who presented me with a teak statue of a Korean farmer and a gentle note of thanks. I think of G. Rodriguez, who handed me a funny self-portrait with the inscription "Odd Man Needs Love Too." I think of V. Vinas, who ended the autobiography I assigned him, "That is my life, my poor Puerto Rican life." Few of its former clients have prospered.

Literary Limbo
(1985)

This was written five years ago, while I was awaiting publication of my first novel, Maud Gone. *It seems so ingenuous, sweet, sad, and long-ago to me now. My excitement for my poor book. The hope that I could ever make a living at this trade. And imagine! Calling writers "witty folk"!*

Since this article I have gone public, with two novels and these essays. I have revealed myself, in fact and in fiction, to be a person who would consider an abortion under certain circumstances, who knows about sex, and who, in fact, likes it; who has seen a psychiatrist, who has had doubts in the past about her sanity, and deep-rooted on-going doubts about organized religion, the Pope, the medical establishment, heaven, marriage, our country's foreign policy, and sometimes about men. Also, I have some facility with four-letter words.

The people I needed to worry about turned out not to be just the older generation. There are friends, relatives, of my own age who have not approved. I know of some by their silence. Others spoke.

"I got your book, but I didn't get to read it because then I had to take it back to the library."

Q: "Is it smutty? Is it just for married people?"
A: (From a defender) "Yes, it's just for married people."

Q: "Have you read Kathy's book?"
A: "I read enough."

"If she calls this writing, she'd better stop it!"

191

But some people overwhelmed me with their love and generosity.
June Beisch wrote this poem for me when Maud was published:

Of course I'm glad
You're getting your book published.
Why shouldn't I be?
You've had as much rejection as
The rest of us.
You've suffered too.

Now they will have a party
Everyone will be reading and misreading
And manhandling your book.
Some envious writer will say
How did this no-talent
Ever get published?

But it won't matter to you
Because inside—you're changed.
Inside—there's a small part
Already dead. The part that had
To die out like weeds
So you could let the blossoms
Come.

My first novel was accepted more than a year ago. By a good publisher, I was astounded to hear. Two months went by between the acceptance and the signing of the contract. I was worried for those two months because, despite my agent's reassurances, I was certain that my editor had second thoughts. I had been found out. She knew I was a fraud and wasn't

literary enough for them after all. I knew she had told my agent
and my agent was working up the strength to break it to me.

Then, on line for a poetry reading, I met a young lady whose
first novel is also forthcoming. We congratulated each other
and smiled a lot. We spoke up so that others on line might
hear. Then she said she wanted it to be published before her
thirtieth birthday, and had asked her publisher to move up
the date for that reason. And we had been having such a nice
conversation too. I couldn't think of much to say after that,
though I did keep smiling. I didn't hear much of the reading
either, what with Time's winged chariot clattering away behind
me.

Though I am a new writer, I am not a particularly young
writer. I had a wasted youth — fun, but basically wanton. So
now I couldn't wait. When would my editor call? When would
we start? When would we get the show on the road and the
book on the shelf?

"Why the delay?" asked my friend, a corporate lawyer. "If
your book were a brief, my firm could have it published in
a week."

I told her it's different with a novel. I don't know much about
it, but I told her there's editing and proofreading and something
called galleys.

My friend shrugged. "Like I said . . . a week." This didn't help
me much.

Then I got the contract and, more important, the check,
half of my advance. I knew the editors were going to publish
me after all.

Next, my editor called me and explained that she wouldn't
be getting to me for a while. There were books ahead of mine
on her list, and they had to be taken in sequence. And before
the book would be published, there would be discussions,
rewrites, artwork, galleys. Everything takes time.

I suddenly didn't care. A delay in the rewrites might mean a delay of pub date. (You see I'm learning the lingo, too.) I am terrified of whatever pub date holds. I like it here in limbo. Because even though I don't get to sing hosannas, I haven't been banished from the kingdom.

Now I think that it is precisely because I am not in my first youth (thanks for the euphemism, H. James) that I can savor this time all the more sweetly. I see quite clearly that it may be my shining hour. Who would wish it gone?

I've worked for sixteen years as a teacher, and, while I've been fortunate in my colleagues, life had, let's say, its predictable side. No great pleasure, no real terrors. (I work in a good school.) I liked the safety but I craved excitement. You see here one facet of my neurosis.

The rest of my psyche will be laid bare when my novel is published. It's autobiographical in the way of many first novels. Publication means exposure, and that could get chilly.

There are people who may leave me when the book comes out. People I've known from infancy; people who have loved me in their fashion. My novel isn't outrageous, but it is honest, and I have never been honest with these people. I could not be and still have them.

The real me is in my book. The adult. The writer. They are proud of me now. They've never known a writer before. But I fear that they will leave. Who needs them, then? Who cares? I do. The real me. The child. The writer.

My story will be on the street. Everyone will know my shame. Everyone will know my name. Or worse, maybe they won't. Maybe only my family will buy it and see how I've embarrassed them, and for what?

Right now my parents are still proud of me. My child still gets invited to birthday parties by children of nice families.

I haven't gotten us evicted as undesirables from our apartment. The old ladies on the elevator still smile and greet me.

My husband hasn't gotten fired because he is the spouse of a deviant. In fact, he actually tells his clients about me, a practice that alarms me greatly. I beg him not to, but he does. He's our sole support now that I've taken a leave of absence to Write. Doesn't he know how important his job will be when my principal decides that I'm not a fit example to my students? He says no, that I'll be supporting him soon. He says he believes in me. Which is why I married him in the first place.

My daughter likes my life as a writer because I am around more. I can pick her up myself from kindergarten and take her to Baskin-Robbins. I don't grouch as much when I clean her hamster's cage. We don't have to leave as early: she gets to watch cartoons these mornings. "I'll have to go back to work soon," I tell her. "This time off is just for a little while. I have to go back and make some money."

"Your book will make you money," she replies. "and it will make you famous." I never told her about famous except to say that it was what Michael Jackson was. I told her this once when she asked about limousines. I told her that rich and famous people rode in limousines. Michael Jackson rode in limousines. Is this what she expects of her mother?

My old friends still like me. They tell me they want to be invited to my publication party. I tell them they might have to throw my publication party. A friend's dermatologist says he'll buy my book, so there's that sale, at least. Someone else says she'll take my picture for the book flap—she has a new Polaroid. Another offers me his family for my next book. (We writers don't work that way, I tell him gently.) My cousin from California took me out to dinner when he was in town.

Also there's a way of telling who your friends are. People I thought were my friends have inquired after the sales of my book. Don't they know it's not on sale yet, that it's not even a book yet? And if they thought it was at the bookstores, why didn't they go out to purchase it and find that it wasn't on sale yet? Huh, I say to myself, and I think I am right in saying it...I don't think the people who said that have any intention of ever reading my book.

But I have new friends to replace the ones who weren't really. I have literary friends, other new writers who send me postcards of Walt Whitman and Virginia Woolf. They call me up and we go out to lunch and gossip literately. I go to readings now. I even gave a reading. A lovely old club has given me privileges for a year. I've been invited to a few literary parties.

I had been invited to these parties before, but it was different. Before, my whole approach was "I'm nobody, who are you?" What I found out was, nobody likes to be nobody too. In all honesty I didn't love hanging out with the other nobodies who would have me. People would ask me what I published. I would tell them of my short story in a literary magazine. They, even the other nobodies, would move on. One fellow put it this way before moving on: "Would it take less than a half hour to read your entire published works aloud?" I like it. It was stern, but a little different, and definitely up front.

Literary parties were kind of tough on me because I'm naturally gregarious and have always enjoyed regular parties. I always brought this expectation of having fun along with me.

Ah, but now I am having fun! You don't just go to a literary party to make a report, but there is that element. If you report well, you get to stand there and casually chat with witty folks, with writers, with the people you have always wanted to be. I can't say I don't like it, because I love it.

My reporting has been going well. I make modest mention of my novel. People say, oh, and congratulations, what a fine publisher, and, what is your name again? I tell them, again.

I have told some of them my name each time I've seen them at a party in the past, but I'm glad to tell them again now. I like saying my name. I think that this time they may remember it. At least until the review comes out...

It's like an E.F. Hutton ad. Someone nearby says, excuse me, I just heard...And I graciously repeat my name and accept congratulations. It occurs to me that one could work these parties for a year or so without having gone to the trouble of writing a novel.

I think, in a few months, if my novel is still not out, I'll change my approach a bit, talk about my current project. So far, though, no one's eyes have glazed over.

I have seen this syndrome, the glazing over of eyes. It is horrifying. It is brought directly on at the mention, by a writer, of his work, published only a year ago, unsung and unread.

They ask me when my novel will be published. I say soon, but I'm not sure when.

★   ★   ★

My rewrites are done now. My editor calls to say they're fine, and that the copy editor has my manuscript. Things are really moving. "Great," I tell her.

The Bomb, the U.N.,
and I Turn Forty
(1985)

*The U.N. and I are still around, if a bit older and more tarnished.
The bomb, too, is somewhat diminished. It is slated, as it had initially
been, to arrive at Staten Island, (cozily coded "Homeport") in the
summer of 1990. But the Navy has been forced to make cuts, and
the battleship* Iowa, *which was to have been Homeport's cynosure,
has been mothballed. That means 4,000 sailors will not be coming
to Staten Island, considerably lessening a beneficient economic impact
on that borough. Still scheduled are six nuclear-capable support ships.
But because of the cutbacks, these ships would have to be taken
from other ports, and those ports are starting to protest their loss.
Also, there is serious lobbying against Homeport, and at least eight
congressmen have signed a letter of protest to Secretary of Defense
Cheney. For the record, I'm still against it. Home is where nukes
aren't.*

I am as old as the United Nations. I am as old as the bomb.
I was born into fragile new peace at the end of a long and tragic
war. I will be forty on Election Day, 1985. On my birthday
ballot is a referendum, the first voter-initiated referendum in
New York City in nearly two decades, intended to block a
Navy base on Staten Island for ships capable of carrying nuclear
weapons. Forgive me if I wax apocalyptic. People turning forty
act a little funny. I'm beginning to think my life is inextricably
bound to the bomb.

Mayor Koch is against the referendum. He says that voter approval of the proposal would be "to the eternal shame of New York." Citing the existence of a large naval base in San Diego, the mayor asks, "Are the lives of Californians in San Diego less valuable than lives of New Yorkers?"

I do not think so. I believe, truly, that the individual life of a San Diegan is every bit as important as the individual life of a New Yorker. Life is high on my list of things I believe in. There are, though, so many more lives in New York than there are in San Diego.

Is this the question? Must we really be thrown into competition with San Diegans for *life*, as if there weren't enough of it to go around? Shouldn't there be enough life if it is let to live?

I can see the beginnings of a good David Letterman riff here, out on the streets with a minicam, asking New Yorkers the question: "Do you think New Yorkers are worth more than San Diegans?" (To be fair, Mr. Letterman would look for New Yorkers who had actually been to San Diego and met San Diegans.) We wouldn't have to stay up late—we already know the responses from our fellow citizens:

"Does Howdy Doody have a wooden anklebone?"

"Would I get up in the morning if I didn't?"

"C'mon, ask me something hard!"

The mayor's question stayed with me. It reminded me of something. Then I realized. It was another question, one I had been asked often on my way to forty: "Do you think you're better than Lizzie Dean?" The nuns asked me that whenever I got uppity. It could have been Lizzie Dean or any contemporary that they thought I thought I was better than. That, or such variations as "What are you, conceited or something?" Because I wanted more. Because I wanted too much. When I got too old for other people to ask it, I asked it of myself.

"Did I think I was better than Lizzie Dean?" Finally, about in my thirty-second year, I saw the question plain. It is one designed to keep a person in her place. "To hell with Lizzie Dean," I said, and the saying of it freed me up a good deal. Lizzie Dean would have to make her way without me.

I'll bet Mayor Koch made this decision at some point, to get on with things and not worry about whom he thought he was better than.

I think this about worth. It cannot be compared. It comes from within. And very often one's worth in the eyes of others comes from the worth that is within. I don't know that this is the way it should be, but in my forty years I have observed it to be true. And this: a person who walks forth secure in her own worth is often emulated.

Not long ago I read about a man who, while he had no comment on San Diego, seemed to think New York was worth a lot. George Steiner, the author and critic, told the Royal Society of Arts in London that New York was ". . . the empire city, which imperiously lays claim to being the capital not of its country, but of our current climate of modernity." He went on to say, "Like no other city before it, it [New York] is a democracy of hope." And: ". . . no other city on the planet today poses so many decisive questions as to our future."

His words echoed what a woman told me years ago, over a pint in a London pub. "We look to New York," she said, "to see how it will be for us."

Supporters of the referendum say that such a base on Staten Island would make all New Yorkers participants in the arms race, and New York a prime target in the event of a nuclear war. I believe that New York is already a prime target in the event of a nuclear war. Who among us has not seen the ominous chart of circles radiating from the Empire State Building, the epicenter, out from the epicenter to our seashore and our mountains? The Empire State Building has been the epicenter since I can remember, before any talk of the Staten Island navy yard. I went with my family to the top of the epicenter last Christmas Day. We stood among the festive crowd and looked out upon all that would be destroyed, though our eyes could not even see to the first circle. I can see the epicenter from the playground as I push my child's swing, rising tall and grey and majestic behind our much lower building, behind her laughing face. I do not mind so much living in sight of the epicenter. Of the bomb, my mother always said, "If it falls, I want it to fall right on top of my head." She said it doing simple things, changing a baby or brewing a pot of tea. She said it to me because I was the eldest.

What I mind much more is the part about making all New Yorkers participants in the arms race. "Somebody has got to stop it!" my husband said last week. He was talking about social convention, dinner parties and such, but it applies. I decline. New York now has an opportunity to decline. New York declines. New York is not willing. New York sends regrets. New York, secure in its worth, the capital of modernity, is laying its imperious claim on this very decisive question as to our future. Not eternal shame, but glory, temporal perhaps, but still radiant, would crown us. New York could be a true democracy of hope, even for San Diego.

We have the United Nations and so are doing our bit for world equilibrium. There are those who say the U.N. is a symbol merely. So, we fervently wish, naval bases to be also symbolic. The U.N. is a more worthy symbol to represent a democracy of hope.

Mayor Koch warned from the deck of the *Intrepid* that if it isn't safe to have this base in New York, it's not safe to have it anywhere, leaving unilateral disarmament the only alternative. This is such a heady, exciting idea of the mayor's, a domino policy for peace! One city after another sending regrets around the world.

"Love of country is involved here," said the mayor from the *Intrepid*. "I'm not in any way disparaging the patriotism of those in opposition. I'm saying they're absolutely blind." His disclaimer to the contrary, I believe that he was disparaging my patriotism. A Mr. Greg Leo of the Federal Immigration and Naturalization Service recently disparaged Mayor Koch's patriotism when the mayor spoke out for the illegal aliens in our city. It's hard, getting your patriotism disparaged.

I remember when you were younger too, Mayor Koch. You were my congressman when I first came to this city. You stood tall on my corner and shook my hand. You were wearing a black ribbon on your lapel, a protest against a war.

I turn forty beside the epicenter. I feel falsely young and reckless, never far from laughing or crying. If age means how many years you've got left, I may be as young as my daughter, as old as my mother, for we may die on the same day of a most unnatural cause.

Springtime
for the Homeless
(1988)

We had a beer in the Gloccamora, and, when we stepped out, were surprised by the late light of a day we thought was dark. A shoeless man had unzipped the filthy ski jacket that had taken him through the winter and was speechifying from a plastic webbed lawn chair on the corner of 23rd and Third.

"He has a point to make," said Claude.

"Ya–ay, let's all get out the lawn chairs!" said Denise. Things, obviously, were fine in Gloccamora.

Hey, and things are great out here too. Spring has come to New York City after one hard winter. Praise! Praise...whom? Some of us are reluctant to ascribe praise after what we have seen, but we feel, nonetheless, an inchoate gratitude rising with crocus and Celsius. Praise.

Because, for a little while at least, the homeless aren't homeless anymore. Naw, really, it's true—they're just... camping out!

And we homebodies can doff the guilt along with our winter coats. Because isn't outdoors where everyone wants to be these days? I mean, if you didn't have responsibilities and have to waste your substance in some dumb *office* somewhere.

Am I right? Wouldn't *you* like to be outside today, maybe at Pete's, sucking back your first gin and tonic? Aren't you just dying for *Rigoletto* in the Park? And the Seaport on Friday nights again! It's spring, goddam, and we can enjoy it purely, because for a few months anyway, the birds of the air, the lilies

203

of the field, and the homeless of New York have chosen the better part.

Now when you buy your homeless person (you do have your own homeless person, don't you, like everyone says they do?) his morning Blimpie Sausage n' Egg w/coffee, can't you almost smell the open campfire? Don't you wish you could just plop yourself right down there next to him on the subway steps and belt out "Val-er-ee, Val-er-a-ha-ha-ha-ha-ha-ha," or maybe skip work, cop a token, and take the train all the way to Coney Island?

Some bleeding hearts are going to whine: "But it's so crowded out on the streets." I have no patience with such benighted statements. Where have these people been? Even if they haven't been to Banff or Yosemite lately, they're sure to have heard the horror stories. Hey, face a few facts about our world. It's crowded everywhere.

Others will beat their breasts and say: "But they don't have tents." This is projection pure and simple. The speaker is obviously such a candyass camper himself that he thinks the homeless can't hack sleeping under the stars. It must be emphasized that inner-city camping is the most rigorous of recreations. It takes the body and psyche to limits well beyond the demands of Outward Bound.

Still, the bleeding heart's attitude must be faced squarely if he is to enjoy spring fully. If this matter of tents is all that's holding him back from his hey-nonny-no-ing, I suggest he take his homeless person on over to Tents & Trails, EMS, or Paragon and get him some gear.

Outfitting the homeless for camping need not be that costly. I like the G.I. mummy sleeping bag, which can be had for $89.95. The Kwik Cook Stove folds flat for easy carrying and burns sterno...$3.95. A 7-oz. can of sterno is $2.95. Used government-issue army tents are only $6.95. And do invest in a drop cloth, only $8.50 for a 6' x 8'.

Homeless families present a greater challenge, of course, but a Camouflage Family Dome can be had for $90.00. (An added feature: if we put them in camouflage, maybe we won't see them anymore.) The Casa model is adorable, sleeps three, and has the advantage of being four-season...$89. For when *mi casa no es su casa.*

Even if you can't go the whole route, why not tuck a few freeze-dried food packets, a Splash-Lite (he can hang it on his key chain), and a Swiss Army knife into a Padded Pak'r ($19.95) and drop it off at your homeless person's corner? A cute way to say "Happy trails to you."

What if you don't have a homeless person? One very good suggestion I've received is go to Port Authority, where you're *sure* to find one, buy him a ticket, and put him on the bus to Freeport, Maine, so he can do his own shopping at L.L. Bean.

Spring gets a lot of bad press—Eliot calling it cruel, and Edna St. Vincent Millay with her "To what purpose, April, do you return again?" Not me, I say seize the day. Let New York be Fun City again for just a little while...because summer's coming. Yes, I agree. Summer *is* a great time for camping, but by July some of our inner-city campers who've been at it for a while start getting these tans that are a little *too* good, you know what I mean?

But maybe by then we'll be able to stop busting our chops and get in some camping of our own. Think it's too late to reserve the site we had last year on Prince Edward's Island?

The End of the World
(1990)

If I haven't learned to love the bomb, I've certainly gotten nostalgic for it. It seems so quaint these days, the notion that there'd be a second Big Bang to call things off. So symmetrical. So quick and clean.

I've known all along that the world would end. You are protected from sex going to Catholic school, but you find out about a lot of the lesser evils. When God told Noah after the Flood that he would never end the world by water, he left himself a loophole. He never said he wouldn't end it. Just not by water, that's all. Up until now it's been guesswork as to just how he would effect the demolition.

Sister Agnes had her version and let us all know in third grade. How the sun would come crashing down on us, causing darkness and flames everywhere. How the dead would rise out of their graves with their Fu Manchu fingernails and long long hair, wearing frayed do-rags and winding cloths. How there would be the stinging of serpents and the howling of a great wind that would only fan the fires. You wouldn't be able to find anyone that you knew, only God, with the good on his right and the doomed bad on his left. There would be a clock above the doomed, ticking "Never-ever, Never-ever." Sister Agnes paused for emphasis and fingered the dark beads on the huge rosary hanging from her waist. The beads shone from use, and looked like large poison berries.

She told us about the weeping and gnashing of teeth that would ensue. Everybody would be weeping and gnashing, even the righteous who were about to enter heaven. That was what alarmed me the most, the profound desolation of the righteous, in whose number I certainly planned to be. That even they, and I, should not be spared this heavy sorrow! Why would they, of all people, be carrying on so, when they were going shortly to a far better place? I knew why: they would miss the world. I knew how much I would.

That afternoon I went next door to the convent where I took piano lessons from Sister Cecilia. I went into the practice room to do my scales and warm up while Sister Cecilia worked with another pupil in the next room. Instead, I put my head down on the closed piano and wept. After a few minutes Sister Cecilia flew into the practice room on her voluminous sleeves, whipped me five times with her pointer, told me to stop crying, called me a lazy stupid girl, set the metronome going to four-four time, and flew out. I silently condemned Sister Cecilia to God's left side and began to practice "Papa Haydn's Dead and Gone" to the resolute, relentless metronome.

As I grew older and lost my faith, I realized that Sister Agnes's account was a kind of fairy tale you tell to children, like Santa Claus or the Easter Bunny. It was meant to comfort us and shield us from the truth, which was the bomb. It was a metaphor for the bomb. The bomb was how the world would end.

The bomb was even worse than Sister Agnes's story. It had already arrived, for one thing. It had already been used. Its destruction of the world was imminent. And though there was a bomb that would destroy only living things, there was none that would make a distinction between the good and the evil among us. Deaths by the millions. Melting flesh and eyeballs. Birth defects and mutations. Nuclear winter. And we had done it to ourselves, not waited around for God to cut the sun loose.

To protect us from the bomb, my father and the handyman dug a hole in our backyard and tunneled into our cellar. They lined it with cinderblocks and filled it with Campbells Pork n' Beans. We would be safe there. We would be safe crouched down under the cafeteria tables at school, our hands over our heads; we would be safe in the bomb shelter Dad built.

I remember my backyard, and the buttercups that grew there. Remember buttercups? Do your kids know that little game, holding the flower under your chin to see if you like butter? Remember butter? Remember daisies and "He loves me, he loves me not?" Do your kids ever do that, lying on their backs on a hill somewhere? Like other games, you need the equipment. Remember making daisy chains?

We swim in a lake in the summer. It is getting choked by Eurasian milfoil, a particularly tenacious weed that laps up phosphates from dishwashers. When we were young we could swim out clean and straight. Now the kids have to take a tube to get out past "the ickies." They don't complain, since this is what they know. I try not to complain either. (I never tell children about the good old days when there was no milfoil and only the bomb. They would hate me!) Our lake is, otherwise, a lovely lake. And the nearest lake to it is much ickier. It has human feces in it.

But even if you have to swim with shit, you're luckier than most. We brought a child, call her Sonia, to our lake. She couldn't swim. We outfitted her with a lifevest and tire tube and she splashed about rapturously. I wondered: Why can't she swim? "Where have you been before, Sonia? The ocean? A pool?" I asked. Sonia lay back in the tube and stretched her hands languuorously over her head. "Nowhere!" she yelled, and kicked away from me to her friends. Sonia is ten years old and landlocked, or, more precisely, concretelocked. She lives in Manhattan near one of the latest water main explosions, the one that spewed asbestos into the air and nearby buildings, requiring men in space suits to evacuate the buildings and drape them, Christo-like, in white.

It's autumn. Say you feel like taking a drive out to get some zinnias at a farm stand. It's Sunday, why not? Just by *yourself*? Not with a carpool of people? Go ahead, go all by yourself on such a frivolous mission and send up carbon dioxide emissions that will find their way to the growing hole in the ozone layer over Africa, where you don't yet have to buy flowers, you can still pick them, and where most people can't afford food, let alone cars.

Once, long ago, it was only the bomb. Now it's everything: your styrofoam cup, your hairspray, the asbestos in your hairdryer, the electromagnetic rays in your electric blanket and your bedside clock, our hospitals burning hospital waste. On New Year's Eve 1990 I kissed my child and said, "It will be a great decade." I was putting on a good front.

"Oh, do you really think so?" she asked.

"What do you mean?"

"You think it will be so good, with oil spills and homeless?"

★　　★　　★

When I left Sister Agnes's tutelage, I began to learn from the poets, who seemed to be at least as concerned with the world and its outcome as she. The situation had Wordsworth depressed at the beginning of the nineteenth century, and we're talking about a time when it was still possible to see ten thousand jocund daffodils at a glance:

> Little we see in nature that is ours;
> We have given our hearts away, a sordid boon!
> . . . Great God! I'd rather be
> A Pagan suckled in a creed outworn
> So might I, standing on this pleasant lea,
> Have glimpses that would make me less forlorn.

T.S. Eliot knew all along, but I didn't understand, really, until recent years:

> *This is the way the world ends*
> *This is the way the world ends*
> *Not with a bang but a whimper.*

Edna St. Vincent Millay was talking about a man, not the world, when she wrote: " 'Tis not love's going hurt my days,/But that it went in little ways." Still, it expresses my peculiarly wrenching sense of loss. She's also the one who wrote, "O world, I cannot hold you close enough!" Me either, and I feel the pain of its leaving every day.